THE
THRESHOLD
OF CIVILIZATION

WALTER A. FAIRSERVIS, JR.

THE
THRESHOLD
OF CIVILIZATION

✵

An Experiment in Prehistory

Charles Scribner's Sons

New York

Copyright © 1975 Walter A. Fairservis, Jr.

Library of Congress Cataloging in Publication Data

Fairservis, Walter Ashlin, 1921–
    The threshold of civilization.

    Bibliography: p.
    1. Man, Prehistoric.   2. Civilization—History.
I. Title.
GN741.F34   901.9   74–14892
ISBN 0–684–12775–X

1 3 5 7 9 11 13 15 17 19 V/C 20 18 16 14 12 10 8 6 4 2

Printed in the United States of America

To Jano

Contents

Illustrations

MAPS

Preface

THE STUDY OF PREHISTORY is ultimately concerned with the genesis of civilization: how man's remote past led to the origin of that way of life whose complexity man has struggled to encompass ever since its origin some five millennia ago. The evidence consists largely of the artifacts of daily life, especially those tools and weapons concerned with the finding and the preparation of food. Consequently many attempts at reconstructing prehistoric life are dominated by scenes of naked or seminaked individuals crouched over a fresh kill or squatting by a campfire gnawing at the foodstuff which modern interpretation accredits them with obtaining. Such scenes, however, deny prehistoric man the cultural sophistication which must necessarily have existed if civilization was to emerge from an essentially barbaric way of life.

Archaeologists, particularly those trained in anthropology, are attempting a review of their interpretative techniques in a concerted effort to discover the true place of prehistory in the evolutionary development of man's cultures into civilization. What follows on these pages is one such effort. It is an experiment that goes beyond artifacts and makes no apologies for flaws large or small which are naturally inherent in an experiment. The interpretation of the evidence of man's remote past poses one of the great challenges to the reasoning mind. The acceptance, however, of that challenge is not an ivory tower exercise, for there is a consequence in human understanding of vital meaning to mankind's future.

As the subtitle indicates, this work is an experiment in prehistory. Part One presents a theoretical frame of reference by which certain key case studies are reviewed in Part Two. The result may provide material for arriving at a more precise definition of civilization—and may indicate why civilization is with us at this time in our history, whether we like it or not.

Thanks are due to my research staff at Vassar—Suzette Chu, Elizabeth Walters, Elizabeth Ann Miller, Lynn Gordon, and Eleanor Bookwalter—and to Miss Walters and my wife Jan for drawing some of the maps and illustrations. In connection with the illustrations, I am grateful to Professor Robert J. Braidwood, the Oriental Institute of Chicago, for permission to use material from the Jarmo excavations, and to Dr. James Mellaart, Institute of Archaeology, London, for permission to reproduce the Çatal Hüyük material. The Vassar College Research Fund and the Department of Anthropology of the American Museum of Natural History provided material support at critical times.

THE
THRESHOLD
OF CIVILIZATION

Introduction

THE SPREAD OF EGALITARIANISM throughout the world has been impelled by the concept that, given his "natural" freedom, man will develop his true nature, which has always been essentially good—that oppression has made man bad and caused his fall from grace. The opposite view—that man is essentially bad—sees history as a struggle to create structures through which the good might be nourished until it would be strong enough to change that fatal flaw in man's character.

For a long time thinking men have believed that the rise of civilization was demonstrative of man's success in overcoming his savage nature. The institutions of civilization known as the arts have moved man far from the unthinking barbarism of the past. Today, confronted by a civilization which appears to have run amok, many people would argue that "civilization" is only another name for an ever more terrible barbarism. This view is reinforced by a greater understanding of the life of those very primitive peoples whom the West once spurned and labeled "savage." The Pygmies sing to the trees, the Bushmen enjoy their "hard" life, and the Hopi and Zuni reject Western "civilization" out of hand—an act which becomes increasingly attractive to the bewildered urban man. As similarities are found between the life of modern primitive people and those who lived in the remote prehistory which was the prelude to civilization, civilized men may well wonder whether the rise of civilization has not indeed been a descent into hell.

The concept of civilization has been defined in so many ways that understanding the term depends upon one's knowledge of the definer. The term has its root in the Latin *civitas,* which meant "state"—with special reference to the presence of cities. The words "city," "citizen," and "civilian" all come from the same root, implying that the concept of civilization is closely connected with the concept of city life. What Winston Churchill termed prehistoric civilization might more accurately be described as prehistoric culture, since he was referring to a time when there were no cities.[1] Anthropologists generally adhere to the Latin meaning, characterizing civilization as either urbanization or a cultural phenomenon of which cities are a symptom.[2]

This concept of civilization may seem remote from that used by writers who see civilization as an ideal, a culmination, or a level of consciousness. Freud was an exponent of this view:

> Civilization is a process in the service of Eros, whose purpose is to combine single human individuals, and after that families, then races, peoples and nations, into one great unity, the unity of mankind. . . . And now, I think, the meaning of the evolution of civilization is no longer obscure to us. It must present the struggle between Eros and Death, between the instinct of life and the instinct of destruction, as it works itself out in the human species. This struggle is what all life essentially consists of, and the evolution of civilization may therefore be simply described as the struggle for life of the human species.
>
> [It is] my intention to represent the sense of guilt as the most important problem in the development of civilization

and to show that the price we pay for our advance in civilization is a loss of happiness through our heightening of the
sense of guilt.[3]

Freud's idea—that civilization for all its fruits has caused
man's loss of an essential freedom—permeates the writing of another great student of civilization, Lewis Mumford. Mumford
finds that the onset of civilization objectified life and made property and power more important even than life itself.[4] Regimenta-
tion and coercion are the instruments by which civilized "good" is
achieved and maintained. The American anthropologist Robert
Redfield (1897–1958), a leading student of the folk order of
human society, concurred in part in this view. He saw civilization
as the culmination of an evolution of mankind towards institutionalization and the impersonal application of a moral order which
had been the personal, often unstated, and collective ordering of
life for primitive man.[5]

The societies of primitive man are virtually extinguished when
they come in contact with civilizations. Civilizations act with violence upon the noncivilized because civilizations demand resources
and are dynamic entities undergoing cycles of change from primitive beginnings to classical climaxes and eventually painful ends
marked by cultural decadence and extinction. This thesis of civilization as an evolutionary phenomenon pervades the writing of
renowned historians from Gibbon to Toynbee. Violence, coercion,
aggression, and exploitation are as characteristic of evolutionary
civilization as are innovation, peace, education, and acts of reason. Civilization in this sense is like a biological organism, the
result of natural selection—simply another adaptive phenomenon
in a biological world of challenge and response.[6]

Yet civilization is often equated with an ideal state of life. The
philosopher of history Alfred North Whitehead (1861–1947) stated
this view succinctly:

The notion of civilization is very baffling. We all know
what it means. It suggests a certain ideal for life on this earth,

and this ideal concerns both the individual human being and also societies of men. A man can be civilized, and a whole society can be civilized, although the senses are somewhat different in the two cases.

I put forward as a general definition of civilization, that a civilized society is exhibiting the five qualities of Truth, Beauty, Adventure, Art, Peace.[7]

Other writers have seen civilization in a similar light—in its best sense, a model for the world. Ralph Waldo Emerson, Rudyard Kipling, John Ruskin, T. S. Eliot, Clive Bell, and the art historians Bernard Berenson, Herbert Read, and Kenneth Clark, for example, suggest in various ways that civilization is ultimately a growth of perception, a refinement of feeling, taste, and understanding; they each relate it to a term such as ''civility''—the quality that distinguishes the civilized human being from the barbarian and is civilization's most distinctive feature.[8]

One of the most profound interpretations of civilization has been set forth by the historian R. G. Collingwood, who saw it as basically a mental process moving towards an ideal condition in human relations—civility.[9] The concept of civilization as a stage in man's history—as described, for example, by the American historian George P. Adams—makes Collingwood's interpretation particularly significant.[10] For man has not only evolved in his ability to deal with the physical world in terms of its material existence but is learning to perceive the laws, orderings, and ideas which underlie all being—in other words, of existence beyond the mere sensuous.

In the third millennium B.C., in the developmental period of early Egyptian civilization, the priests of Ptah, in Memphis, had already conceived of idea as an abstract of their god's action. Every creative thought and motivating action of man was believed to originate as an idea of Ptah's. In Mesopotamia, in the celebrated Sumerian epic of Gilgamesh, the hero questions the need for human mortality and in so doing probes the cosmological basis of man's sensuous existence.

The Jesuit paleontologist Pierre Teilhard de Chardin (1881–1955) distinguished the self-realization which man has reached—the noosphere—as in effect the outermost layer of the world's revelations. It is the all-encompassing layer of thought which has its best expression in the achievement of civilization.[11]

All concepts of civilization beyond the mere material definition assume that the appearance of civilization means that man has reached a level of world perception and understanding more acute than in any previous time in his existence. Such features as an improved technology, securer economic system, a complex social organization, the production of cities, and the appearance of writing might be regarded as the result of man's growth of cosmic awareness and not the other way around. It is assumed, in other words, that the idea came before the reality—but how might one prove it?

One method is to study how the observable criteria of a civilization came into being. Such an approach characterizes the studies of experimental science made by the American chemist and educator James B. Conant, of Harvard, the studies of the theoretical basis for scientific change made by Thomas Kuhn, and the speculations on the political implications of scientific theory made by Arnold Brecht.[12] Other such studies have focused on the evolution of art styles, the rise and fall of civilization, the influence of great men, and the effect of conflict. Worthy and important as such studies are, they are usually concerned about origins only as a kind of hindsight. The fact is, however, that in terms of man's total history civilization is a late phenomenon—little more than five thousand years out of the quarter million or more of human existence. What precipitated civilization? What sustains it? Where is it going? A hint of the answers to such questions may well be found in the vast stretch of prehistoric life which led to civilization.

If civilization is to be defined, however, by more than the presence of certain tangible, perceptible objects, how can the archaeological evidence of prehistory—which consists largely of such objects—be used to arrive at that definition?

In recent years anthropologists have studied the genesis and growth of civilization with increasingly greater interest. After almost a hundred years of research into the lives of primitive people, anthropologists have arrived at a series of axiomatic concepts applicable to any of man's cultures, no matter how complex. Because anthropology is uniquely equipped to deal with civilization as simply another culture (although "simply" is hardly the word), anthropologists can review modern and ancient civilizations in a manner previously unavailable to historians, philosophers, sociologists, and other traditional students of civilization. This is possible because there has never before been such a large body of substantive data upon which to draw for an understanding of *all* human behavior. It is clear that new understandings of civilization will emerge.

Everyone who has ever seriously attempted to define civilization would probably agree that the civilized state of mind is a result of the whole of human behavior, not just a part of it. It is the attempt to explain this whole behavior that marks the anthropological approach to civilization and promises specific exemplification of what till now has largely been a vague awareness.

As one wanders the streets of civilization's cities and views human behavior within them, it becomes abundantly clear that not all people who claim membership in civilization are civilized. Acts of pollution, aggression, and illegality can be seen at every hand; a kind of blind senselessness pervades behavior as if some people were marionettes guided only by the strings that lead from raw emotion. Yet such people manipulate and are affected by the things of civilization: motor cars, newspapers, television, medicine, standardized clothes. A question arises from such observations: Are those who use the products and plans of civilization civilized because they are capable of using them or is "to be civilized" something more? After all, the simple Pygmy can be taught to drive a car and read a magazine. Is such learning the equivalent of civilizing? Is a man civilized because he can read or drive a machine?

Prehistoric man passed through several stages of cultural development, as will be demonstrated in the pages that follow. This development was evolutionary in character and involved factors of natural selection of a kind found in the development of a growing child's adaptation to an ever-enlarging world. Conceptually the whole child grows in awareness and capability until he can take his place in an adult society as a recognized responsible participant. There is an analogy here that may go far beyond mere simile, for if the true achievement of civilization is indeed the equivalent of prehistoric man's coming of age, then the definition of civilization involves all the mature factors which make up one's understanding of adulthood. This wholeness includes both mind and body and is as concerned with the ideas that make things possible as it is with the things themselves. In effect, a civilized individual possesses a mature mind in a mature body, as was noted long ago in classical Greece.

It is a premise of the following chapters that prehistoric time was like the infancy and childhood of an individual, a period when man, already possessed of natural physical capability, passed through stages of intellectual awareness until he reached that stage of self-consciousness called civilization. This suggests an answer to the question posed above: Some men achieved civilization in the past and passed it on as a potential for all individuals; it has not, however, been accepted by all individuals even though paradoxically all individuals live within it. Many people who are adult in body have not intellectually recapitulated the prehistoric experience essential to all civilized human beings and accordingly still remain within the grasp of the material world from which the truly civilized have long since been liberated. The implication for our times of such a thesis is very great.

Part One

IN SEARCH
OF CIVILIZATION

SO GREAT IS the mass of archaeological and ethnological evidence available to the student of man's remote past that the student's problem is not to find new evidence but to develop some scheme by which to interpret the existing evidence. Scholars have set forth a number of such schemes, most of them characterized by a strong element of economic determinism—in keeping with the emphasis of modern times from Marx to Galbraith. The scheme developed in Part One of this book emphasizes an aspect of psychology as the basis for an interpretation of man's prehistoric prelude to civilization. Paradoxically, however, it is anthropology which provides the foundation for that interpretation: a necessary condition in the ongoing search for civilization.

I

The Two Visions
of Man

THE VALLEY OF THE NILE inevitably invokes a sense of timeless-
ness: the essential unity of past, present, and future; for Egypt
reflects in its monuments, its villagers, and its land the fact of a
present so rooted in a past that the future is apparently made
secure. The hoary Sphinx and the ancient pyramids evoke a spirit
of wonder that men could build monuments as enduring as the Nile
Valley itself. Past accomplishment validates and reinforces human
spirit in the present for the sake of the future.

   In the cold light of present-day realities such contemplations
seem romantic fancies, the usual poetic musings of those that
"drink of Nile waters," but they may not be. To regard past
human endeavor as merely a foundation for present endeavor is to
assume that the past of man is simply a series of almost identical
stages like the stone blocks in a great building, all essentially the
same but cut differently according to location and function. Modern man can point with pride to an incredibly complex technology
which enables him to live longer, travel farther and faster, communicate easier, and exploit the physical environment more readily

than in any period of the past; still, one may wonder in these tense days how much men have accomplished in terms of true human happiness, how many believe in an essential human morality directed to the ultimate good of all life as found in the ancient creeds. There is a modern tendency to regard human history as simply a history of the evolution of hardware which has imposed its own rationale, paradoxically serving man while enslaving him. In such a view, man is only a kind of imperfect computer evolved by natural selection, created by the challenges of technology, whose brain finds truth only as a consequence of the mathematical logic called science. In keeping with this view, the world's schools decreasingly educate the young in art, music, philosophy, poetry, literature, human history, and increasingly in mathematics, physics, chemistry, economics, and psychology. The graduates of an American high school have academically in common only years of arithmetic and mathematics. Modern answers to world problems are essentially mathematical answers: development is economic development; peace is the result of armed equality. The landing by man on the moon is so linked with technological achievement that only about 25 percent of the American population knows the name of the man who first stepped onto the lunar surface—as one can readily determine by testing one's neighbors.

The dread vision of a material universe, soulless, meaningless, responding only to material instrumentation, stands before the modern world, and the modern world's citizens—increasingly trained to accept such a vision—respond in kind, believing that the taxonomies and systems conjured up by mathematical logic are the demonstration of ultimate laws by which man must live and die.

Biologists have shown that man is the product of a material universe; he has evolved with all organic life on earth and is superior to other organic life only in that his particular adaptive capacities give him exploitive advantages other organic life does not have. This unique and wonderful capability is the direct product of organic, material evolution which in the total history of evolution has no particular direction except toward greater organic complexities. These biological "facts" have become a credo for modern man. It is man as the animal—the evolved primate whose behavior brings about his own suffering—that the modern world is concerned with: cage him in planned utopias, surround him with hedonistic devices, train him collectively, manipulate his genes, drug him—the solutions fly from the human computers.

Every man sensitive to the history of the world must find that there is within himself something that rejects this materialistic vision—something that does not comport with mathematical truths. Opposed to the materialistic vision is another vision, which holds before man the promise that all that has happened and will happen leads eventually to something better. According to this vision, human history represents a total evolution of all parts of the human entity: individual life, society, culture. Unlike the identical blocks of materialism's view of history, the nonmathematical history is cumulative: each stage divests itself of something which impedes man's progress to the eventual good; each stage is witness to new awarenesses of that good; each stage adds something upon which the next stage can be built: Human evolution has creative meaning not only to man but to the whole earth and perhaps beyond.

The two visions confront each other, and no compromise is possible. Which is the true vision? There is no direct answer, but there is more than a hint that human history contains one if we but learn to understand it.

The Egyptian Evidence

In the course of two field seasons at the site of Hierakonpolis in Upper Egypt I had reason to climb the cliffs which lie to the west of the site. Hierakonpolis is the Greek name for ancient Nekhen, the presumed seat of Narmer, one of the founders of dynastic Egypt. Narmer's town is now referred to as the Kom el Ahmar, the red mound, because of the accumulation of reddish pottery and burnt earth which marks the ancient habitations whose eroded remains form the mound itself. Excavations in the Kom el Ahmar in the latter part of the nineteenth century produced some of the most famous art works in Egyptian archaeology, including the Narmer palette and the copper statues of King Pepi. A magnificent gold hawk's head was also found there. This precious object represents the god Horus, patron god of all Egypt, son of Osiris and Isis, the divine parents whose myth recounts the triumph of life over death. Horus of Nekhen is the probable prototype of that son of immortality, and it is under his aegis that Narmer conquered all Egypt and united the two lands, some thirty-one hundred years before the birth of Jesus. Our excavations found not only the remains of a building which could well have been Narmer's palace but much evidence for the later periods when Egypt's capital was Memphis of the White Walls and the Old Kingdom pharaohs were constructing the pyramids. An inscribed stone reused later as a door step evidenced that a temple, whose mudbrick walls we had revealed by scraping, was constructed by Thutmose III, well known as the creator of Egypt's largest empire a thousand years after the pyramids were built. In an alleyway nearby an inverted pot concealed the tiny skeleton of a human infant who lived in the Pyramid Age; a lotus offering made twenty-five hundred years later to the hippopotamus god Hapi was depicted on a small stela found in a hutment in the midst of the imperial temple. The dating of the stela was helped by its association with some pottery of the Graeco-Egyptian heirs of Alexander.

The Kom el Ahmar is situated in the midst of modern cultivation some three hundred yards from where the Libyan Desert begins. Along that desert edge for hundreds of feet are found the remains of the habitations and the graves of the predynastic people led by Narmer and his predecessors across the threshold of history. The place is strewn with the bits of flint, pottery, bone, shell, and ash which is all that remains of the life of a people whose aggregation at Nekhen was vital to the creation of the most ancient Egyptian state. Through the midst of this windblown remnant of remote life a waterless riverbed leads from the green cultivation to a gap in the desert cliffs a mile or so away. As one follows its course through ancient silts deposited when ice covered much of the northern hemisphere and the seas of the world were hundreds of feet lower than now, one sees upon those silts an ancient brick structure—the earliest still-standing brick building of its kind—built by a pharaoh a dynasty after Narmer, symbolic of royal power still represented in the Nekhen home of its genesis, though as distant in time from that genesis as the Pilgrims of Plymouth are from the present. A rocky hill nearby is pierced with the tombs of nobles of an age when Egypt was torn from the security of the moral order of the Pyramid Age; when the pharaoh as the son of the sun god, the living Horus, bridged by his presence on earth the shadowy line between mortal and immortal, joining Egypt so closely with its gods that they were one and the same. Four thousand years ago Egyptians questioned traditional ways and faced the mortality of man, discovering that man's grief was owing to his own misdeeds and not the vagaries of the gods. The tombs by the dead river proclaimed the old formulas but simultaneously evidenced that another spirit was in the air—the concept of sin and its consequences. Still farther along the river course, where the cliffs cast their shadows as the sun sinks, prehistoric men had their settlement nearly six thousand years ago. Their stone, fired clay, and bone and shell artifacts lie scattered about in fragments among the hearths which were the physical center of their households. There was more rainfall then, and where the river debouched from the hills small ponds were formed and catfish lived in them. Ostrich shell and the bones of ungulates evidence that the surrounding desert was a grassland like that of East Africa when the great game herds roamed free. These prehistoric men shared a few artifacts with the men of the desert edge, proving perhaps an ancestral relationship.

Above in the cliffs, if one looked from the Kom el Ahmar to the west, are the long-ago-looted tombs of nobles of the early days of Egypt's imperial role in the ancient Near East, when Egyptians—made warlike by the challenges brought by foreign conquerors from Asia—invaded Palestine and Syria and brought the Sudan into an imperial hegemony of states. It had become clear by this time that the gods of Egypt could not be localized in the Nile Valley; they must rule the known world. But the citizens of that varied world did not acknowledge Egyptian cosmology, for they had their own gods, one of whom—Yahweh of the desert people— forbade the worship of any other god. Egypt, unable to absorb foreign concepts or to reconcile them with its own, fell back on repetitive ceremony to promote its ideas on man's place in the universe. In the end ceremony elaborated by wealth, power, and paraphernalia became empty, and Egyptians gradually returned to the soil—except for one brief interlude when a cult of the sun god given a voice by a believing pharaoh, Akhenaton, proved that some Egyptians entertained concepts of world order beyond the established and practiced views.

Along the ancient river course, among terraces which mark the beaches of monstrous Pleistocene Niles generated when the waters of Africa poured in flood northward to the Middle Sea, one finds the worked flints of men who lived by the Nile hundreds of thousands of years ago and were preyed upon by long-extinct creatures of Ice Age Africa. These were the men who, using their dexterity of limb and mind, made possible the survival of human children beyond their long infancy and, by that peculiar bonding of parents and children which marks the human family, insured a human future.

High on the cliffs of sandstone laid down by primeval seas in the Age of Reptiles one overlooks the whole course of the dead river: its dendritic head extends kilometers into the desert—a waterless region of nearly two thousand miles of sand, gravel, and denuded hills extending to the Atlantic Ocean. One stands on the cliffs and looks westward as far as the eye can see into the desert—a place of heat, wind, and mirage—but the sharp eye notes here and there a man-built pillar or a heap of stone which marks the way to some oasis sanctuary en route to the heart of Africa—to Lake Chad, to Kordofan, or the Mountains of the

Moon. To men of the past the desert was no barrier but a way to the beyond, to salt, to skins, to ivory, to dwarfs, to apes, to spices, to gold—the exotic stuff which promises to fulfill the yearnings of human appetite.

From the heights it is always to the Nile Valley that one must turn. The green cultivation conceals the great river in its midst and makes the desert mountains across the valley even more desert in appearance. The scarred cliffs have openings in them—the tombs of nobles of imperial Egypt. For when Nekhen died as a center of pharaonic Egypt a new center was created across the river—El Kab, the ancient Nekhab, populous trade center in the heyday of Egyptian empire. Here the Nile ships blown southward towards the great marts at Elephantine 60 miles away stopped to pick up Egyptian produce and passengers; the Nile ships carried northward by the current plied their way to Thebes of the hundred gates and beyond, carrying the produce of Africa as well as befeathered and bejeweled envoys from the land of Kush to bow before the reigning pharaoh. While one wonders at the splendors of El Kab, the smoke from a railroad locomotive suddenly rises in the distance above the date palms. The railroad runs from the Mediterranean to the gates of the Sudan. It flourished in the days when the British hold on Egypt appeared to weaken after Gordon died at Khartoum. The undaunted Englishmen who returned to the Sudan brought their army by rail from Alexandria to the now-submerged Wadi Halfa and then across the desert to a point where ship, horse, and camel could do the rest of the job—and insure the conquest of the Sudan. At Omdurman near modern Khartoum the last great native African army fell before the modern rifle, still waving the ancient spears and swords whose use antedates the very founding of ancient El Kab.

Power lines cross the desert below the cliffs bringing electrical energy to Cairo from Aswan. Two great dams at Aswan create a lake whose waters now cover Nubia, a land where ancient Egyptians, Copts, and Arabs found treasure, sanctuary, and exile in often strange and varied ways. Nubia has always been an enigmatic land—a passageway to inner Africa, a barrier to civilization, a homeland for many. Its bitter lands, fatal to the unprepared or to the weak, have been magnetic and vital to those who could see them truly.

Of all the features in the landscape, natural or man-made, the most impressive is the Nile. Along its shores the fellahin raise water by the same shaduf their forebears used thousands of years ago. The bound reed huts, the growing fields of wheat, the date palms, the cattle, the goats, the birds, the laughter, the way of thought have hardly changed since before the time of the pyramids. Nile boats move by sail or current, their placid courses occasionally diverted by a Hilton Hotel tourist boat or a motor-driven barge.

Here human history is wondrously encapsulated. Does that history have special meaning? Which of the two visions of man does it support: the aimless selections of biological evolution and terrestrial materialism or the thrust towards a superorganic purpose eventually utopian and boundless? James Henry Breasted (1865–1935), founder of the Oriental Institute of the University of Chicago and America's first Egyptologist, saw in the ancient Egyptian experience a harbinger of an age of character yet to come. The English historian A. J. Toynbee found the Egyptian experience demonstrative of the cyclic destiny of civilizations: to rise and fall according to historical principles. For the ancient Hebrews Egypt was the heartland of despotism; for Napoleon it was the keystone of an imagined empire of the East made vibrant by *la gloire*. In Egypt as everywhere man's visions confront one another and there seems to be no solid choice among them.

The Presence of a World View

It is undeniably true that man the product of organic evolution has uniquenesses that set him apart from the generally instinctive creatures which have evolved along with him. Paramount among these is self-realization. *Cogito, ergo sum.* The self is conceived as more than a sensuous animal but as a possessor of the knowledge as to where one exists in the familiar universe. A universal characteristic of cultures past and present is a world view, a cosmological description of what things are, how they are ordered, why they function, and man's place among them.

The American psychologist J. S. Bruner identified three stages in the development of a world view in the growing individual.[1] Similar stages can be seen in the development of man's cultures, and Bruner's terms (although not used here with the precision that he gave them) can be useful in identifying various stages of cultural growth in the ancient societies to be studied.

The first stage is called enactive, and it is characterized by an almost purely physical understanding of the world. What the individual can touch, see, smell, taste, or hear determines the parameters of his world and his reaction to it. The second stage is called ikonic; it is essentially an image-making period. It is the most social stage since it involves the individual's growing awareness of his place in his society: family, peer group, strangers. The final stage is the symbolic, where symbols representing material and nonmaterial entities become motives for behavior; the individual's actions depend on both reaction to symbols and the ability to create symbols, as in speech. Awareness of the world is thus a cumulative matter, beginning in simple physical reactions and ending with perceptions of symbolic meaning often of great complexity.

If one were to order the world's cultures on the basis of their nearness to the modern scientific view of the nature of the universe, the most primitive groups would be classified as enactive because of their powerful existential conceptions based upon immediacy of relationships to the world about. Agricultural societies tend to be ikonic, with cosmologies that assign superior or inferior status in a stratified universe, parts of which may be personified. A conscious concern with abstract conceptions and the relationship of symbols to those conceptions clearly characterizes modern technological culture. In fact the term "civilization" is often used to label cultures whose idea symbolism involves the use of writing and mathematics. Abstraction is found in all cultures, however, and is the basis of all cosmological conception. Primitive man, for example, attributes boundless energy to all phenomena whether mobile or immobile: a stone has its energy as much as does a deer or the sun itself. More advanced cultures in their personification of the universe paradoxically conceive of action as the consequence of divine forces beyond the control of the divine; civilizations in their turn reiterate the power of idea or the meaning of square root.

Because of man's ability to conceive abstractions, no matter how simply, a world view is always possible, but when that abstraction is symbolized to the extent that it gives explicit direction to human action, it has a consequence in human awareness of self, society, culture, and the universe beyond. Consider the level of abstraction and attendant symbolism in the following quotation:

> Time in the large, open time, takes its direction from the evolutionary processes which mark and scale it. So it is pointless to ask why evolution has a fixed direction in time, and to draw conclusions from the speculation. It is evolution, physical and biological, that gives time its direction; and no mystical explanation is required where there is nothing to explain. The progression from simple to complex, the building up of stratified stability, is the necessary character of evolution from which time takes its direction. And it is not a forward direction in the sense of a thrust toward the future, a headed arrow. What evolution does is to give the arrow of time a barb which stops it from running backward; and once it has this barb, the chance play of errors will take it forward of itself.[2]

For primitive man the arrow analogy in reference to time would be meaningless, since the idea of time is generally limited to present or recent experience, nor would the abstract "direction" be truly understood as something which the arrow points out. Instead, the explicit fact of arrow possession represents the capability of the arrow to do that for which it was created. There is abstraction in the magic potential of arrows as manifestation of energy: arrows can hit or not hit their targets independently of the hunter's will. To this extent the arrow is a symbol of an abstract idea, but its empirical quality sharply bounds its usage. As it is used in the quotation, however, it is simply a symbolic way of describing the intricate relation of the myriad symbols which civilized man has evolved to explain phenomena. In this case the only limits imposed are man's self-imposed willingness or unwillingness to multiply symbols, always, however, with the necessity of making certain that whatever symbols are used are mutually intelligible within at least one society whose symbolic knowledge would permit that intelligibility.

If it is true that men evolve to new and higher levels of understanding and if it is true that, among the living cultures of the world, there is a gradation in the awareness of the universe as science understands that universe, it is also true that the evolution of man's cultures through time was as much an evolution of cosmological awareness as it was of technological capability: the stone ax of prehistory is a harbinger of the jet aircraft or the television set in its demonstration of man's toolmaking capability.

Egyptian history demonstrates with chronological verity the complicating cultural forces which ancient men evolved in response both to the challenges of the physical world and to the dynamic character of the social and cultural environments which men were creating. The prehistoric Egyptian had a limited world view; thousands of years later Pharaoh Akhenaton was conceiving of a universe with an ultimate abstraction at its heart symbolized by a radiant sun which was not alone *the* sun. The pyramids of Gizeh and the new high dam at Aswan are comparable in terms of mass and energy output. Yet the abstraction involved in the ancient Egyptian conception of the pyramid as a place of ascension is a relatively simple one needing comparatively few symbols to represent it. But the incredible engineering feat of damming the Nile for the sake of electrical power depends on a host of symbols meaningful to a multitude of physicists, chemists, engineers, hydrologists, and contractors—many times the number of symbols used by Old Kingdom Egyptians to construct the pyramids. The same symbols used to build the great dam can also be used to describe the dimensions of the physical universe or the nature of a chemical compound. Clearly, as the Egyptian experience demonstrates, much has happened to enlarge man's view of the world.

History reveals, then, a parallel between the growth of cognition in child development, the ranking of living cultures in terms of cosmological consciousness, and the evolution of man and his cultures through time. In considering the question of what man is now and where he is going, it must be a premise that there has been an evolution of man's awareness in the past and that evolution has made man's consciousness of the whole world more acute and his knowledge ever deeper. This being so, it can be assumed that there is a pattern of direction in human cognition which, properly understood, can make man aware of potentials beyond his present ken. If man can establish that there has been direction in his rise from simple enactive levels of comprehension to the teeming complexity of a world of symbols representing the abstract realities of the universe, then the goals of the future come into focus.

To find clues to a possible orthogenesis for man one must begin with man himself, not—as some would have him—simply an evolved, communicative, aggressive, toolmaking primate, but a thinking human being. The distinction is vital, for thought in this context is not cunning or animal skill but the type of reasoning that develops rational solutions to the human condition—solutions that lead to understanding. The argument that human aggression is the result of a reasoning mind locked into a predatory animal is untenable in the context of cognitive evolution. The human mind has certainly made man's aggressive capabilities more fatal but its use in that context is geared to the most simplistic mental behavior possible; to outwit and kill one's prey hardly challenges the human mind. In fact the term "the stupid" is an excellent way of expressing symbolically the degree of mental exercise necessary to hunt, to soldier, or to snarl.

But to conceive of a world where sensuous man lives in harmony with himself, with society, and with the universe at large through the application of reason requires the greatest mental energies men can generate. The symbolic awareness of reason is the highest level of cognition which man has been able to reach; as the French philosopher René Descartes (1596–1650) expressed it: Man the finite could have no conception of the infinite if it were not for the actuality of that infinite. Reason is that apparently ungraspable yet tangible infinite, and its existence in the mind of mortal man, whatever its origins, can hopefully be said to be due to a directional attribute of human evolution.

The remote temporal reaches of prehistory were the setting for the evolution of cognition, but studies of prehistoric man necessarily emphasize his material side, for that side is most evident in the surviving bone and stone which represent him. It is relatively easy to demonstrate a prehistoric development of technology and to argue for stages of markedly different emphases from the wandering days of the primate scavenger to the sedentary stabilities of the Neolithic farmer. Economically determined stages of prehistoric life may also have marked stages in the growth of human awareness, of the development of thought; if so, this tangible prehistory, the preamble to civilization, may confirm a direction in man's cognitive evolution.

2

The Dawn
of Cognition

The Character of Civilization

CIVILIZATION IS THE PRODUCT of man's cultural evolution, the
most complex culture that man has evolved to date. It is generally
believed to have begun in the Near East late in the fourth millennium B.C. The civilized men of the following thousand or so years
laid the cultural basis for the rise of the classical world in which is
rooted the civilizations of the West. Though modern archaeology
has made clear that the early civilizations of India and China arose
independently of those of the ancient Near East, the fact that all
those civilizations came into being within a millennium or so of
one another suggests that all resulted from a response to a common
phenomenon—the complexity brought about by prehistoric settled
life.

In all the ancient civilizations cities arose which became the
centers of those civilizations; centers where government, industry,
and the institutions of ideology had their seat requiring central controls and the produce of an ever-expanded countryside. So dependent were cities on the subsistence resources and raw materials of
that countryside that their citizens used their centralized efficien-

cies to insure that their sources of supply were secure. Thus the cities dominated the land.

Civilizations are never really secure in spite of their organization and their ability to exercise civilized controls far from their urban centers. All parts of civilizations are dependencies: the ruler depends on the ruled, the merchant on the market, the farmer on the merchant, the priest on the congregation, the peasant on the city, the city on the peasant, the state on the army, the army on the state. Yet so complex is civilized life that in spite of dependence most people and institutions interact remote from one another. There is a constant need for representation of the individual or his powers without the need to be personally present. Simple reciprocal barter, for example, is not adequate to encompass the complexity of economic exchanges in which hundreds of different items have fluctuating values.

The life of civilized men and women is fraught with contradictions, for one person's good is not necessarily the group's good and what seems good for the group can often destroy an individual's good. Even the definition of good is a relative matter, and "good" as the basis of law, of individual freedom, or of collective liberty is the subject of much speculation. It is no wonder that early in civilization's development there have appeared the Buddha, Confucius, Ptah hotep, and countless other saints, wise men, and philosophers concerned with defining the proper symbols to guide men along their civilized courses.

The use of symbols for all aspects of civilized living is a property of civilizations. The spectrum of symbolization runs from the signs used in writing and the formulas of mathematics to the devices of religion, politics, and the state. Money or its equivalent is essential to the economic system, as are standardized weights and measures. A person's mark, that is his written name, seal, or signet, is as important to his property in his absence as is his physical body when present. It is through symbols that men record the meaning of "good" and codify their laws. Symbols are seemingly limitless, depending only on their mutual intelligibility among the group. Noncivilized people sometimes use symbols extensively, but none are as dependent upon them as civilized man. It is no wonder that many scholars have equated the beginning of writing with the beginning of civilization, for writing serves civilized men as a mode of communication and of expression in so many ways that it is impossible to define civilization without describing some form of writing.

Symbolism, whether in writing or in other forms, is the product of much more than the simple development of artifactual civilization. It is the result of a capability innate in man: the brain functions not only to supply the immediate needs of the human body but to adjust that body to the social environment. It is this adjustment that makes society possible and permits the complexity of interrelationships that have created the whole of culture: polity, technology, social structure, religion, mythology, world view. At the heart of this innate capability is the ability to communicate by means of sound. Many animals have this ability but in man it goes far beyond the limited spectrum of cries, barks, chatters, and mutters which animals use to announce danger, courtship, fear, and anger. For hundreds of thousands of years men have survived by combining a modicum of running speed, swimming ability, throwing accuracy, and good eyesight with an abundance of cumulative brain power. Because of this power, experience is not lost to the individual, for he remembers what happens in his daily life. Man orally communicates his experience to his society; society can thus share the individual's awareness of environment and build its own collective understanding of cause and effect without having in each case to experience individually the step-by-step sequence of events. Thus the craftsman need not be concerned with how the property of his material was discovered. He can accept his society's prior knowledge and go on with his work—sometimes finding some small innovation which will be added to his society's store of knowledge. Societies through various forms of contact can add their own awareness of the world to that of still other societies. Because of man's communicative ability the history of his cultural evolution is culminative—but by no means regularly progressive. A comparison of the innovations of the past fifty years in the West with the past fifty centuries makes this point clear.

The Appearance of Tool Manufacture

It was during the Early Pleistocene, over a million years ago, that one of the Australopithecine primate forms, now made familiar by recent discoveries in East Africa, began to make tools out of stone, wood, and bone. The vulnerability of a terrestrial primate of apparently no particular outstanding physical capability except dexterity of hand and arm in the variant terrain of East Africa motivated life habits of peculiar kind. This form of Australopithecine was probably no more than five feet in height and must have depended for survival upon an awareness of his own vulnerability. This was made especially acute by the fact that his children took so long to mature—at least ten years before one could aid in the food seeking whose success is the cornerstone of organic life. The need to nurture and protect the young for ten years must necessarily have restricted the female's daily wanderings to a small range, perhaps to a sheltered nook of the East African landscape near water, sources of edible roots, herbs, bark, nuts, and fruit, where careful search would result in finds of lizards and rodents, all of which were prey for these omnivorous primates. The male, drawn further afield in the hunt for subsistence, must nonetheless be certain his family was as safe as empirical knowledge could make it. This also imposed a geographic limitation and emphasized the fact that what was locally available should be exploited to the full. Unrestricted wandering into the unknown was anathema. Studies of primate behavior confirm that the primate troop would rather adhere to reasonably restricted and familiar territories than to roam far afield into the hazards of the unfamiliar.

Territorial conservatism, long infancy, and individual vulnerability added up to selective pressures on that primate species, pressures which were to result in increased and variable forms of social cooperation between families and the maximization of the use of the resources of the inhabited territories. This maximization involved a more effective means of obtaining subsistence than gathering, scavenging, or stalking a vulnerable prey that could be killed by biting, choking, or battering. The primate needed some means of augmenting his modest teeth and muscular power; the means evolved was the tool.

Other primates have used tools, but the deliberate and repetitive manufacture of tools for a variety of purposes is confined to man. Consider what toolmaking involves: a precise foreknowledge of what one desires to make: a sharp cutting edge, a keen point, a shape to fit the hand. Here there is a consciousness of an end—a final form which extends to actual use, a use which vicariously allows the would-be toolmaker to experience that future moment when the form he has created performs its function. In turn the material, the pebble or stick or piece of bone, must be fashioned by learned means of cutting, chipping, or rubbing until out of what was once amorphous the definitive tool emerges. Thus there must be first an idea for a tool, based on empirical understanding of its potential use, and then a step-by-step sequence: finding the raw material, manufacturing (in its own sequence), and the actuality of the finished tool. In toolmaking, then, man conceives a form and imposes that form on the external world. In this sense the finished tool is as much a means of communication as is the spoken word, for its presence and utility are mutually recognized by all members of the society.

The Origin and Meaning of Speech

Speech requires almost precisely the same mental processes as toolmaking. There must first be an idea and then a step-by-step sequence: a series of sounds which result in images or meanings understood by the individuals who make up the group. Meaningful sounds spoken in sequence by an individual are thrust into the world where the audience hearing them gains understanding of the individual's idea. It is probable that language grew from the ability of early men to name things and to describe in sequence the actions connected with what was named. Naming is a complex matter. It is not merely labeling. The word *lion,* for example, involves both the individual's and the group's understanding, not only of the appearance but of the behavior of the lion. Indeed the term can invoke group and individual experience with lions and cause physiological reactions of a dramatic kind. Furthermore, naming classifies; *lion* has taxonomic validity, for it differentiates that animal from other animals and helps order the world of animals in the mind of the individual and his group. The word *lion* also collectivizes the hunter's group, for the term invokes common understanding of lion capability as against, say, that of the giraffe.

One aspect of naming that has enormous importance to an understanding of man's unique place in organic history is man's naming of members of his social group. In some primitive societies an infant is not named until it has proved it can survive. Naming is delayed in numerous societies for more than a year and when it occurs it is attended with due ceremony—often much more elaborate than that carried out at the actual birth. In Western civilization, however, baptism most often occurs within the first year of the child's life. There are provisions for christening the newborn by laymen when there is danger of death. One of the basic factors in the controversy over abortion in many countries of the West lies in the idea that once conceived the embryo is already a living individual and needs only its sex determination to be ready for a name. The idea that an individual could live in the world nameless is inconceivable in most of the world's societies.

Naming within human society differs from the naming of objects outside the group, for it involves the conception of self—not sensuous self alone, that self that is driven by biological mortality to eat, drink, sleep, cohabit, struggle for survival, and respond to hurt or pleasure, but the self which has identity in the group as one who responds to his fellow human beings in those myriad ways which constitute personality. Naming may start in individual life as a means of identifying an individual, but in time a name adds up to more than physical existence: a person's absence does not impede the conjuring up of the individual in the mind's eye when that individual's name is spoken. What is remembered is most often not mere physical appearance but personality, the dynamic attribute of being. In the human concept of self the individual views his place and that of others in the society and in the world according to age, sex, occupation, talent, and personality. Accordingly the world's societies, whether primitive or civilized, are extensions of each individual's conception of self collectively manifested in the characteristic human relationships which make that society cohesive. Differences are largely due to adaptations to the natural environment and to the ways in which society makes individual self-conception conform to that of the group. To think—to say "I am"—in human society is to assert one's identity as more than a biological animal: an identity which secures one's place as a self-aware, thinking entity in a self-aware, thinking society.

For many scholars, therefore, the appearance of tool manufacture over a million years ago is evidence for the beginning of language and of thought as men use it. As tool manufacturing became complex so did language and thought. It is certain that advances in technology made possible a more secure physical existence and provided a foundation for the existence of larger and larger groups of men. It follows that the larger the grouping and the more interaction among individuals, the greater the need became for an ever larger spoken vocabulary to handle the more complex circumstances of daily life.

Language is not only communicative and identifying; it is evocative as well. Since it results from thought, it evokes thought. There is a significant anomaly in human relationships summarized in the fact that some people are naturally more perceptive, more intelligent than others. Sometimes perception and degree of intelligence can be sharpened and raised by training and education. Differences in age and experience work against conformity in level of thinking acumen. Ideally men seek to understand one another, but increased understanding in the group does not mean uniformity of thought. There is always an imbalance in knowledge among individuals in any society. Language acts to balance this inequality, but in so doing it tends to emphasize the differences in level of thinking or at least the differences in thinking concern. The hunter trying to outthink his prey has a thought process of a kind which emphasizes the empiricism of tracking, stalking, and killing. The shaman considers the signposts of supernatural intervention in daily life and his consciousness of more than what meets the eye calls for a characteristic thought process and equivalent vocabulary. So it is with the old man remembering an experience and the young man desirous of having one. Each speaks as he thinks and there is no assurance that complete understanding comes about from their conversation. Similarly women are by no means thinking identically with men when expressing thoughts about life. Language complexity is the direct result of thought complexity brought on by the challenges of communication among the members of a group; as long as there is a social group, whatever its conformist technological level, there is a factor for the evolution of thought.

At the present time, great efforts are being made to reverse this process. As egalitarianism has moved across the world and mass media have become more and more important as both an informational and a market device, so vocabularies have been simplified. In the United States since 1900 some 3,000 words have been dropped from regular use in the spoken vocabulary. Technical and slang words are of course always subject to changes in usage, but many words were dropped simply because they were not palatable to a people whose vocabulary has to be simplistic if common understanding is the goal. Even the complex technology of our time depends upon such simplistic words as *hardware* and *jet* to lull people into believing they understand it. The modern elite takes refuge in mathematics or in jargon—language that is unintelligible outside a limited group. Abbreviations like "DNA" are used commonly by mass media as if they were words of themselves and

conveyed true meaning which of course they do not. The great gap
that is opening between science, philosophy, the arts, and the mass
of the world's people is in large part due to the fact that institutionalized learning and the mass media have deprived people of the
language ability to express the complexity of thought which modern times evoke. Thus young people use such expressions as
"like," "ya know," "ya see" as interjections in their speech to
cover their inability to say what their teeming thoughts motivate.
The psychological consequence is difficult to estimate, but it is
certainly more dire than the publicized use of drugs or alcohol as
props for the bewildered.

Culture and Cultural Evolution

Tool manufacture, the development of language, and the
growth of human thought all contributed to the creation of culture,
the sum of all human behavioral activities. Culture is at once a
structure and a font of energy. It is structure in that it comprises
the standards a group of people have evolved and live by in terms
of their leadership, social relationships, economics, technology,
and beliefs. (The American anthropologist G. P. Murdock has
found that there are at least seventy elements common to all cultures. All cultures have universals in their structural character
however they differ in their cultural or energizing style.) [1] It is a
source of energy in its formulation of the interrelationships through
which the individual and society have freedom to act and through
which the individual can adapt to both the physical and social environments in which he finds himself.

Both the structural and energizing functions of culture are subject to an ultimate awareness by each individual of what is happening in his world. Each culture's structure sets the bounds beyond
which the individual cannot go and still retain his citizenship in
that culture. The individual is born into a culture and is made to
learn just what the bounds of his culture are. He learns from his
parents, from his peers, from authority, from the exemplification

of daily life as its empirical nature is forced on him. His learning results in a comprehension, a practical knowledge which he uses to adapt to the changing condition of life from childhood to death. For Pygmies the forest is friend, the plain is enemy; for Bushmen the forest is enemy, the plain is friend; for the ancient Sumerians and Greeks death was an end, for the Hindus and ancient Egyptians it was mere transition; for many peoples of the world the moon, stars, and planets mark human destiny; for Western scientists those celestial bodies are interesting physical matter. Thus it is with all aspects of cultural life. One comprehends one's world according to one's cultural bounds. The quality of a cognitive level differs according to cultural form, and thus the ranking of contemporary cultures according to world view is a direct expression of cognitive level and character within that level. The power to symbolize gives civilized men the greatest cognitive capability of all mankind, past or present. The ability to describe and to some degree to understand a physical universe in terms of millions of light-years, quasars, black holes, nova, and relativity ranks side by side with the theologian's proof of the existence of God as undertaken, for example, by Teilhard du Chardin. Through his evolving awareness of his capability, civilized man has learned to change matter, encompass energy, arrest death, feed the multitudes, and struggle against his aggressors. This awareness is directly due to the growth of cognition from those far days when the conjunction of technological invention, language development, and thought complexity began the process. But for many primitive cultures it can be said that their cognitive level is closer to that of prehistoric man than it is to that of civilized man, a factor of enormous meaning to the prehistorian.

Cultural evolution in human history has by no means been uniform. It is as if civilization with its rapid far-reaching evolution was motivated in a special way. For cognition, though bound by cultural limitations, is not a passive phenomenon. The differences in human intelligence, the interaction of differing cultures, the variety of human experience within each cultural unity challenge the traditional cultural bounds and eventuate in change. Every culture undergoes change; whether or not a culture can sustain change and still retain its traditional premises depends upon what is changed, the degree of change, and the rate of change.

Change is of course an adaptive matter. The study of cultural change is an important one in anthropological investigation. In its simplest terms, cultural change occurs because traditional ways of behaving no longer suit new circumstances. These new circumstances can vary from the use of better weapons by enemies to the recognition of new ways of viewing the supernatural. Cultures can accept or reject new circumstances in a variety of ways. Sometimes change is forced on them, as when a primitive culture comes into contact with civilization and its members are forced to wear clothes, be vaccinated, stop headhunting, settle into farming, accept Christianity, and live in quonset huts. Such forceable change usually ends with the impoverishment or annihilation of the primitive culture. Change is sometimes a matter of stimulus, as for example, when the Japanese in the nineteenth century resolved to modernize rather than be colonized or when the Plains Indian of North America adopted the horse after witnessing its use by the Spanish. Change can be caused by trade, war, tourism, evangelism, or individual genius. In each case the culture accepting the change eliminates those older ways of behaving directly affected by the change. If those older ways of behaving were fundamental in the culture, that culture can be said to change its original structure; cognition gains new bounds, for the cultural perimeters are changed.

When left on their own, primitive cultures change slowly, if at all, for they tend to reject or move away from that which would change them. Civilized cultures change rapidly, for the heterogeneity of the daily activities of their citizens, their large number, and their dependence on extralocal sources of raw material continually present innovative challenges. Accordingly, primitive man's cultural cognition is a relatively stable matter in which original mythological explanations of the world have long endurance.

Civilized men have a dynamic, often speculative consciousness of their world. This consciousness is as changing as is the form of the civilization at any given time. Ancient Egyptian civilization, for example, lasted nearly three thousand years with an enduring world view, traces of which still are found among the fellahin. Ancient Sumeria, on the other hand, lasted less than fifteen hundred years and the Roman Empire less than a thousand years, while the modern civilization of the West has hardly begun. The temporal durabilities are less dependent upon political success than upon the civilized citizen's awareness of the original premise upon which his civilization is based. When Augustus tried to reform a changing Rome, his literary support was Virgil's *Aeneid,* which sought to reconcile the old republican virtues with the new spirit of the Greek and Oriental worlds which the Romans were conquering. In the United States an agonizing struggle goes on to adapt the viewpoint of millions of immigrants to the founding vision of the country. In both cases the future of the national culture depends upon the citizen's awareness of both tradition and the times in which he lives. The fact that civilized cultures change rapidly imperils that awareness, and civilized citizens struggle to establish stability in their world view by devising laws which according to their methodologies are intended to be universal: laws of gravity, thermodynamics, supply and demand, gospel, human rights, are expected to remain constant no matter what cultural change occurs. But these ''laws'' are universal only insofar as the citizens' cognition admits them, and that is entirely dependent on the preservation of the cultural structure or at least those structural elements of it which sustain the concept of the laws.

Civilization is then a cultural situation in which human cognition is constantly changing because civilized cultures are constantly changing. Cultural change, being adaptive, is evolutionary. It follows that changes in human cognition are also evolutionary, which leads to the critical problem of civilization itself: Why have civilizations evolved in the first place? Why were the stabilities demonstrated by the existence in our time of cultures not differing in great degree from those of earlier ages overthrown? Why did there appear on the earth a form of organic life which has produced an instability called civilization more potentially diastrophic than that which shaped the earth itself? Why has civilization produced the most dynamic cognitive patterns of all man's cultures— ever-changing cognitive patterns permitting a world view in which the infinite is recognized and material universals provable by finite means can be established?

Again, if one is to find answers to the problem of civilization, one is forced to seek the factors that brought it into being—factors that are perhaps more evident in a study of the remote past than in a review of civilization per se. Civilization emerged, perhaps like a biological sport, after a million years of human existence. At some point in the prehistoric existence something happened which gave direction to what was to follow.

3
The Stages
of Cognition

The Nature of Culture

IN ORDER TO ENTER the wilderness of man's prehistoric past with reasonable hope for finding the origin of civilization, it is necessary to have some kind of guiding idea. This might be supplied through a further examination of the concept of culture.

Culture as the sum of all human behavior can be viewed as a sphere. The vertical axis of the sphere represents the temporal aspects of culture, what anthropologists call traditions. The horizontal axes are the interrelationships of all the parts of the culture at any one time. Thus for any part of a culture there is a tradition and a position which relates it to all other cultural parts. Culture is then a unity of time and space given identity by the factors which make all its parts adhere. For example, a shoe is a shoe because in our culture there is a tradition of leather footwear identified by the term *shoe*. Shoes have a character at any one time which we call a style and that style emphasizes the place of leather footwear in the part of culture which relates to costume.

Anthropologists call the smallest cultural units *traits,* and traits can in turn be compared to atoms in molecules in that they cluster in certain ways to form complexes and systems. A *complex* is structural. Costume is a trait complex made up of traits such as shoes, pants, shirts, and skirts, which in sum form that part of culture called clothing. The manufacture of Western clothing and its marketing can be called an economic *system* of American culture. From this example it is clear that both the complex and the system are mutually dependent and accordingly cohesive. Clothing, manufacturing, and marketing also relate to other systems and complexes. By means of these link-ups all parts of a culture are inexorably tied together. The American economist Wassily W. Leontief emphasizes this point with his analytical input-output charting of the American economy: one part affects all other parts, and what happens to one has its influence on all the others.

Anthropological analysis of the cultures of the world reveals not only that all traits, trait complexes, and trait systems interrelate to the cohesiveness of a culture but that each has a tradition of itself which through time has led those traits, complexes, and systems to their present interrelationships. Thus archaeologists in their findings of ancient cultures have unearthed evidence for more than the artifacts of those cultures. Each artifact is an example of a trait in a complex or a system. A stone ax, for example, is a trait unit in an economic system as well as an exemplification of a stage in the development of a technological complex. In turn both economic and technological complexes and systems relate to other parts of a culture such as the social organization, leadership, and ideology. Since all these parts together prescribe limits to the individual's cognition, it can be said that any archaeological find is a potential clue to the character of the whole culture. It is this which has drawn greater and greater attention to the work of anthropologically trained archaeologists.

It is inconceivable that any culture could be understood without critical attention being paid to its traditions as well as to the way all its definable parts interrelate at any one time in its history. Tradition, being temporal, is not only a measure of how long the part has lasted but reflects the changes it has undergone in that time to bring it to its present condition. Whether a cultural part has changed rapidly or slowly, so long as it has remained a tradition it has evolved; that is, it has undergone a process of cultural adaptation which reflects man's use of that cultural part under the varying circumstances to which the whole culture has had to adapt through time. Because of differing historical and structural circumstances, no two cultures are alike, but there is a vast uniformity in their evolution because of a limitation as to what kind of change can be made. Shoes will probably always require certain features such as soles and fasteners, whether they be simple sandals or high-buttoned shoes with spats. Furthermore, in the evolution of footwear the direction taken is towards more complexity. It is axiomatic that a cultural part has its simplest structure in its beginnings; as it evolves it becomes more and more complex until it either suddenly reverts to its simplest form again (usually as a result of sentiment) or disappears as a result of cultural selection. But its evolutionary direction is towards greater complexity. It *cannot evolve backwards* any more than *Homo sapiens sapiens* can evolve back into his primate ancestors however he resembles them.

All parts of a culture are evolving, but not all at the same time or at the same rate or for the same reasons. The fact that there are primitive cultures and civilized cultures existing in the world even today is indicative of the fact that not all cultures have evolved towards civilization. Toynbee once treated noncivilized cultures as ''arrested'' civilizations, assuming that all cultures if left to their own devices would achieve civilization—civilization thus being the ultimate goal of all the world's peoples. Anthropologists have shown that this is not the case. Cultures are adaptive mechanisms, and their differences are not because of their stage of development in the direction towards civilization, but are rather a mark of their success in adaptation to their special physical, social, and cultural circumstances. Some circumstances required the development of civilization if the cultures concerned were to survive as an entity; other circumstances motivated the development of Pygmy and Bushman cultures.

To say that cultures differ because of evolution explains what has always been true in cultural evolution. The fact of greatest importance here is that some prehistoric cultures did rise in various stages to a level where civilization precipitated out. Since cultural evolution is not a uniform matter but specifically involves the temporally different development of each of the parts which make up a culture, it is obvious that in comparing cultures, even different civilizations, there will be great differences in the level of evolutionary development according to the parts of the culture by which one measures the differences. For example, that whole complex of cultural parts which can be summarized as the techno-economic sector of American culture is obviously at the most complex stage compared to other cultures of the world. Yet in ideology, that intricate cultural sector which describes man's faith and belief, America may be at a simplistic level as compared to Burmese or Pygmy ideology, and the same can be true of social organization.

Some analytical scheme is needed by which to measure the evolutionary level of each part of a culture and at the same time to set forth an estimate of the evolutionary level as a whole. Since cognitive level among cultures is a direct result of the kind of cultural structure present, there is a basis for such a scheme in the three-stage development of cognition: enactive, ikonic, symbolic. An arbitrary sampling of traits, trait complexes, and systems as categories in which to list level of development would produce an arrangement such as that shown in Table 1 (Appendix). Here nine major cultural sectors have been chosen, within which cultural parts have been listed according to this three-stage developmental scheme. The choice of cultural parts within each sector is arbitrary and could be considerably enhanced, but the three cultural models that emerge can be regarded as reasonably representative.

Enactive Culture

An enactive culture typically exists in a small territory, perhaps not much beyond a 40-mile extent in any direction. The territory includes or is related to bodies of water, though the residents may camp elsewhere in the landscape, a landscape which tends to be in tropical or desert regions. The population of the group can vary from ten or less to a hundred. Both the birthrate and the death rate are high, and life expectancy is less than 25 years for both sexes. Population density is less than 3 persons per square mile. Shelter tends to be of the type that can house all the members of the group under one roof.

The individual in an enactive culture finds his principal role within the family. The child learns by imitating the adults. His vocabulary is limited in total number of words, his speech is accompanied by a great deal of gesturing. Analogy, comparisons, and naming are some of his reference categories, and the bulk of his reference is in terms of the recognized environment—the environment to which he has an immediate relationship. In addition to gesture and oral speech, he may draw pictures as a means of communication.

Enactive community is familial in quality, reaching to the band level of social organization. Within the group there is a high degree of tactile advance and response: petting, holding, slapping, hugging, touching, even interadult hand feeding. Enactive social organization emphasizes adult male residence; that is, a wife joins her husband's family. Men and women are equal in status, and there is a decided moral obligation among members of the group: all must do their share, the usually unexpressed requirement of membership. All members of the group command equal attention from all others; ostracism is the fatal price of individual failure. Success in the daily tasks gains temporary prestige for the individual and reinforces his identity within the egalitarian group but gives him no power over it.

Leadership is dependent on the personal qualities of the individual—the possession of natural talents that can be employed in a given situation: a hunt, a storm, a death, an entertainment. Enactive societies concentrate their energies on a cooperative basis. These energies are rarely used for aggressive purposes, as nothing is gained and much lost in being aggressive. When aggression does occur it is in the nature of feuding, in which there is a display of belligerence but little permanent damage.

Enactive ideologies are animistic in that the individual relates to things personally. Phenomena are assumed to be living entities or in possession of a living essence. The world view is spirit-centered, and its reinforcement in the group is through the reiterated experience of the individual who experiences events as the result of the animistic qualities of nature. The shaman recounts such events in his healing and prophesying practice and utilizes them in inducing the placebo effect. There is a minimum of ceremonial elaboration in the crucial parts of the individual life cycle (rites of passage). Rationality is based on the individual's immediate cause-and-effect relationship to his environment, both social and physical; what is *now* perceptible, tactile, and present is far more important than the past or future. Men live in the midst of an always existent universe which is a graspable totality. Number is notational and refers to the quantities of things, such as "individual" or "abundant." It tends to be mnemonic and noncumulative in the context of *now*.

Enactive societies comprise hunters and gatherers living on a day-by-day subsistence basis—which does not mean that they are always on the edge of starvation. Quite the contrary: since they have a perpetual relationship to the physical environment, they thrive according to the environment's fruitfulness, and when they flourish they tend to remain—like most mammalian life. Labor is divided on the basis of sex and age, with females tending to gathering and men to hunting. The production unit is the household and the economic exchange is reciprocal, whether in food sharing, services, or gifts. Primarily because the basic pursuits of life are for subsistence, rarely more than 2 percent of the work day or of the population can be devoted to projects not related to subsistence activities.

The technology is nonspecialized, and the tool kit is limited. Weapons and tools related to subsistence activity are paramount and are usually made in one or two simple steps by use of human energy. Metal is rarely used but stone, wood, bone, ivory, and other comparable materials are common. When metal is used it is usually shaped by cold hammering. Transportation is primarily by walking or occasionally floating or swimming. Speeds of 3 to 5 miles per hour are normal for walking, and a rate of 8 to 10 hours per day can be sustained.

Music is generally a simple rhythmic beating on a percussion instrument or on the surface of the ground, though wind instruments may be used to articulate a counter rhythm or a repeated phrase. Music is basically for the whole group and group participation is most common, though talented individuals may provide leadership in playing or dancing. Graphic art is functional in that it is made for a specific ritual or accounting purpose recognized by the group. Tradition has a major role in maintaining the forms of graphic representations. Drama is inherent in the individual narration of stories to the group. Since most of the stories relate to experiences known to the group, there is considerable vicarious participation with equivalent catharsis. Games, when played, are competitive and physical, usually related to skills necessary to the daily tasks. Costume is sparse and often plain; it is used for modesty or insulation. Some ornamentation for both men and women is common.

Less than 10 percent of all the parts that make up enactive cultures are negative, and there is rarely any real irrelevancy. Change is resisted, and where it threatens, enactive societies tend to move away from its source.

Ikonic Culture

An ikonic culture tends to find favorable residence on fertile tracts of land or on the open plain and steppe, often near the shore. Most residence clusters lie inland within temperate or near temperate zones.

The birthrate is higher and the death rate somewhat lower than in enactive cultures. Population density is between 2 and 15 persons per square mile, and life expectancy ranges between 30 and 35 years. The group population size varies enormously from 150 to 6,000, with clusters of 300 the most common. Shelter is permanent, though it may be carried, and usually consists of a number of detached but immediately adjacent houses.

The individual is expected to play a role in society outside his family. He learns the values of that society by precept. Language has a great deal of social reference in its vocabulary, and vocalization with a generally enlarged vocabulary diminishes the need for elaboration of gesture. Since the individual has an obligation to society as well as to his family, he can be said to be a step away from his physical environment. Written communication through a series of mutually intelligible signs is now known to include ideographic symbols and what the American psychologist I. J. Gelb calls identifying-mnemonic devices. This stage is summarized in Gelb's term semasiographic: expressing meanings and notions loosely connected with speech.[1]

The ikonic community can be either a tribe (a form of social organization comprising numerous clans, clubs, and other sodalities) or a village (a sedentary clustering of population with a common social organization). Males, particularly older males, tend to be dominant; property is usually inherited through the male line, and both blood relationship and possession of property are important in the achievement of status, which often compels a loose class structuring. Prestige is gained by success in fulfilling or exceeding the father's social and economic role. Social relations are based on the observance of traditional moralities, for which names are given, such as the Egyptian *ma'at* (truth) or the Hindu *dharma* (that which is right). Because of the emphasis on prestige, some members of the group have inferior status and tend to be ignored by others. Communication in ikonic society is emphatically auditory: gossip, the recitation of precepts, the naming of social form and function, and the heavy emphasis upon the different aspects of social and economic relations are communicated orally. This oral communication is given further emphasis by the lack of an efficient writing system.

Authority is based upon personal prestige obtained by possession of property or by kinship. It can be challenged and often is, so that ikonic leadership must be frequently coercive in order to survive. It is here that ikonic culture has a dramatic expression, for much as a child at the ikonic stage of development creates images of self in the world as a means of perception, so individual leaders are impelled to iterate an image of prestige both for self-identity and for popular acceptance. A coercive leader or chief can collectivize his group's as well as other groups' energies for his own purpose: group need or personal ambition. Since possession of property and personal prestige are often significant factors in ikonic authority, leaders may promote aggression as a means of reinforcing their status. This aggression is usually temporary and may simply take the form of gathering warriors for raiding purposes and then dispersing them afterwards, each having a suitable reward in plunder and prestige. Some warlike clans or societies can, however, be permanent reinforcers of their leaders' status.

Ikonic ideology, while having a strong element of animism, categorizes the universe in terms of deities who are often organized much as the ikonic society. This cosmology is explained in the repetition of a mythology which is often formal and detailed. Elaborate rites are carried out for the various life crises celebrated by the society, and the ritual basis for these rites is the basic relation of man to the universe. Here a sense that phenomena were created as a means of regulating man's actions is implicit, and this is expressed in the reiteration of divinely inspired causes and effects in which normative concepts are underlined. The present is related to the past by tradition, tradition which has divine origins. Time is sensed as being cumulative and it can be cyclic (as in the Indian karma) or linear (as in the Chinese ancestor cults), but in either case the individual has a responsibility to relate past experience to present existence for future survival. The priest, a permanent religious practitioner, carries out the ceremonies, recounts the mythologies, and reiterates the behavioral ethics. He anticipates consequence in man-god relationships. Empiricism creates a workable pharmacopoeia, which may be applied by the priest in the context of ideology. Arithmetic is an attribute of ikonic culture, probably the result of the need for precision in the cumulative aspects of the culture.

Ikonic ceremonies are geared to herding and farming or situations in which surplus is accumulated. Land and livestock are generally the basis of wealth and capital, which is controlled through kin-related inheritance patterns. The production unit is the clan, the multifamily group, but there may be employment of "strangers"—individuals who exchange services for a share of the production. There is a degree of specialization in ikonic society: there may be household specializations, and limited groups of craftsmen may appear. The authority tends to redistribute goods and services when in control but symbiotic relationships and limited trade can be on a familial or sodality basis as well.

Technology has as its basic tenet a sequential pattern of toolmaking so that a single tool may be the end product of numerous steps. Energy sources can include animal, wind, and some water power. Fire is used for the smelting and casting of metal. Transportation speed is at least double that of enactive societies, with animals and sailboats as characteristic means.

Graphic arts are at the archaic stage of expression: Their basic motivation seems to be iconographic representation—narrative or decorative in function and often aesthetically harmonious, as in the vase painting of early cultures of the Near East or the decorations of skin robes among the Yakut of Siberia. Music includes melody, possibly in response to the need for descriptive devices in an image-making society. Professional or semiprofessional music practitioners maintain a musical repertoire, and their functions are often related to dramatic presentations. Drama is ritual drama; that is, its principal purpose is the reinforcement of ideological belief through the performance of ceremonies and the reenactment of mythology. Games of chance appear at the ikonic level—as one might expect in a property-oriented society.

Irrelevancies and negative trait functions grow considerably in ikonic societies. Aggression caused by the coercive opportunity of a leader can be said to be a negative function when it imperils the unity of the culture involved. Change in ikonic cultures is ten times as rapid as in enactive cultures, partially because of instabilities in leadership and the role of individual personal prestige and partially because of a degree of interregional dependency caused by residential permanency, the narrower spectrum of subsistence emphasis, and the growth of crafts.

Symbolic Culture

Symbolic cultures have a historic tendency to eventuate in an almost universal distribution. They tend to be large in territory, which, if not politically controlled, can still be exploited in some fashion. The group is large and can in the urban context run into the millions. Shelter has immense variety for governmental, religious, social, and economic functions. Both birthrate and death rate are lower than in ikonic society, life expectancy is much higher, and populations are therefore larger, exceeding 18 persons per square mile.

In symbolic cultures the individual finds his recognized role as a member of an institution (an organization concerned with a special activity). He learns his role through special and formal instruction. His institutional role has little to do with the physical environment. His vocabulary is large, though often specialized, and uses world-wide reference. Writing is his most effective means of communicating in institutional life and his writing is fully phonographic.

Symbolic society is rooted in civilization and its geopolitical attribute, the state. Symbolic social life is regulated by written law and by a system of established ethics. Society is stratified according to occupation and wealth, and the individual maintains status through power obtained in institutional advancement or through wealth based on money or its equivalent. Inheritance tends to be bilateral, though women are often given secondary roles in institutional relationships.

Because symbolism is so important, with particular emphasis upon writing (though modern mass media should be considered also), ocularity has a greater role than auditory communication, particularly in institutional contexts.

Authority is largely vested in institutional controls, though individual manipulation of those controls is characteristic. Thus government forms, such as monarchy or republicanism, have both individual leaders of varying power and institutional members who represent the form in terms of political parties, congresses, and courts. Thus membership in an institution is vital for the individual leader. Political power in turn is vested in class, wealth, charisma, or force.

Symbolic cultures are basically interdependencies and need greater material resources than are usually available to them; thus they tend to be aggressive and institute organized warfare.

Symbolic cultures tend to monotheistic or agnostic religions. They consider the Deity as outside the perceptible universe, which is man's, and yet capable of influencing it in a variety of ways. Whereas time is considered in its historical linear sense, the time most valued is the present and its impact on the future. Mathematics with its abstract concepts is the basis of rational scientific thought, and phenomena are considered the consequences of natural laws conceived as absolutes. Medical practitioners are often trained doctors who regard illness as owing to physical or psychological causes, both of which are curable by scientifically rational means. The world view in a symbolic culture is of a material and generally impersonal universe into which man was born and which cares nothing for him. The world view is communicated by writers who give it literary expression.

The economic basis of symbolic culture is commerce and industry. Goods and services are distributed through market systems based on monetization. Almost all members of symbolic society gain identity as a member of a specialized occupation. There can be an incredible interdependency among these occupations. The productive units are institutions whose members divide into management and labor. It is characteristic of symbolic culture that few members are actively engaged in subsistence activity.

Technology is highly specialized and largely dependent on the consumption of fossil fuels. Metal is a primary material used in the technology. The speed of transportation ranges from 20 miles per hour to thousands of miles per hour. Standardization of tools is critical to the instrumentation of industry and is highly developed.

Symbolic arts place heavy emphasis upon concepts of beauty. Classic art is therefore an expression of historical concepts of aesthetic ideals when the particular culture has achieved its most symbolic status. Drama reflects ideas as to meaning in life while games reflect the institutionalized individual's ability to comprehend degrees of complexity.

Symbolic cultures tend to lose precision in relating meaning to symbol, and often certain symbols survive historically that have lost their original meanings. Irrelevant traits are therefore found in some quantity. Negative functions are related to a similar situation. The rate of change in symbolic cultures can be a hundred times that of enactive and ten times that of ikonic cultures. As a consequence there is a constant struggle for meaning and a growth in the number of negative structural and processual features as well as irrelevant ones.

Interpreting the Cultural Models

Cultural models are ideals: if one applies them to any culture of the world where reliable data can be obtained it will be clear that no one culture is ever at one level in all its categories; neither is the individual's understanding of these categories. Cultural cognition, like individual cognition, is developmental. The models represent tendencies in cultural evolution, poles as it were. A culture which has a significant number of cultural parts at an enactive level will have a smaller number of parts at the other levels. Its tendency is enactive, and so it can be labeled. This is a qualitative matter, however; a cultural level must be categorized according to cultural parts which are critical, such as kind of economic activity or the complexity of belief.

Civilization as culture at a symbolic level will include enactive citizens, and enactive culture will have citizens whose cognitive level reaches a degree of symbolic cognizance. It is in the nature of man to have such apparent anomalies in his cultures. Nonetheless Table 1 can be a guide by which to appraise the prehistoric world for its clues as to the genesis of civilization. Even a casual knowledge of the prehistory of the Old World indicates that man arose from extremely primitive, enactive beginnings. Such knowledge provides a base line for the three-stage development scheme to rest upon. Civilization as symbolic culture can in turn be regarded as a terminal point, in reference to which evidence from the remote past can be assessed according to the categories provided by archaeology and ethnography.

Lest it be assumed that the three cognitive stages as outlined here are merely a tentative scheme, it should be emphasized that the evidence of prehistory reinforces such a scheme as a valid description of what actually happened. Whatever the errors compounded by temporal remoteness and the flaws of methodology, it is nonetheless true that man has ascended to a level of far greater understanding of his world than any other living creature. The advent of civilization is an affirmation of this understanding and proof of a cognitive development motivated by special circumstances.

Part Two

IN THE PREHISTORIC
WILDERNESS

THE STUDY OF PREHISTORY is now about 150 years old. It has grown from amateur collecting of artifacts and sensational speculations on the "missing link" to a respectable and significant branch of anthropology. Prehistorians today seem less concerned with the meaning of their finds than with the methods by which the finds were obtained. This is symptomatic of the constant search for a substantive and reliable way by which to unearth and interpret evidence for man's past which would be on a par with the scientific methods used by the hard sciences. Quantitative methods of collecting and analyzing data are now normal parts of archaeological strategies, and there is much emphasis upon such techniques as model making, systems analysis, and statistics, so much so that the layman would find it difficult to understand a modern archaeological field report. Nevertheless, as accomplished as the collection of evidence has become, the interpretation of that evidence in terms of living men seems to be at a very elementary level.

In contrast, interpretation of the near past is at a much more advanced level. Ethnographers and ethnologists have been steadily gathering data from still-living cultures and skillfully reconstructing the near past on the basis of the hindsight the extant culture makes possible. This technique of reconstruction is generally labeled ethnohistory. Ethnohistory offers great promise that it will become a full-fledged part of the prehistorian's scientific method, for it offers not only criteria useful in reconstructing past cultures but a vast comparative resource in living or recently demised cultures of all kinds. The way not only to reconstruct the prehistoric wilderness but to follow the winding path through it to the threshold of civilization must rest in man's understanding of cultures which he can still study. Indeed this is the only way.

4
Terra
Amata

The Emergence of Man

STUDENTS OF THAT VERITABLE HANDFUL of fossils which is labeled the "evidence for human evolution" are generally agreed that there are three groups representative of that evolution. The first and earliest is a group of hominids, found largely in South and East Africa, assigned to the genus *Australopithecus*. Australopithecines were small, bipedal upright individuals who appear to have hunted and gathered in troops, as do other primates. Their characteristic habitat was the kind of parkland visible in parts of East Africa today. This habitat brought challenges of a selective kind in which *Australopithecus* had to emphasize cooperation and communication for survival. Not only were there difficulties in hunting the alert ungulates of Africa but there were dangers from carnivorous predators as well. The evidence indicates that part of the Australopithecine response was the manufacture of crude stone pebble tools for pounding and chopping, the use of fire, and possibly the development of language. Plant food was probably the most common foodstuff eaten and there is a suggestion that while males hunted, females gathered. Food sharing is thereby indicated

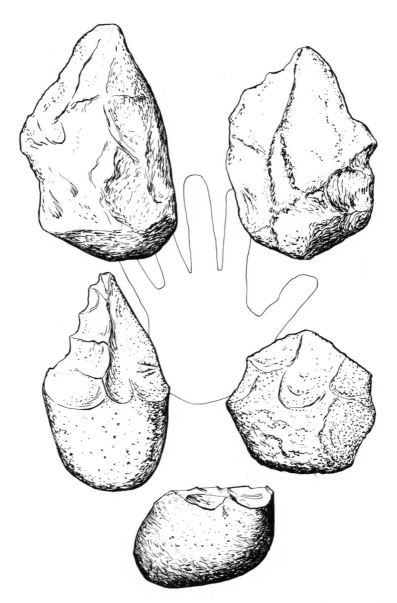

Evolution of stone tools: Early Pleistocene. The earliest stone tools were made by knocking flakes off pebbles to produce cutting or cleaving edges. Those shown here are representative of the pebble tools commonly found at Early Pleistocene sites. Relative size is shown by the outline of an adult human hand (see also facing page).

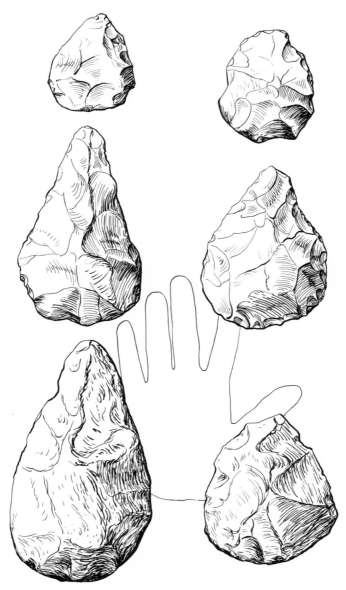

Evolution of stone tools: Middle Pleistocene. An advancement over
pebble tools was made with the development of the hand ax, a
general-purpose tool for cutting (right-hand column) or for stabbing
(left-hand column). The hand ax evolved from massiveness to
slenderness and smallness.

as well as the likely possibility that an approach to the human family was made through permanent bonding between adult males and females and the observance of incest taboos. The Australopithecines were extant for several million years, and in that time their brain volume apparently increased over 50 percent, perhaps an indication of an evolutionary trend towards greater intelligence. Although most human morphologists agree that *Australopithecus* was manlike, few consider him fully man but would place him somewhere in an intermediate position. One important piece of evidence is the rough stone circle recovered by British paleontologist Louis Leakey at the Olduvai Gorge, one of the earliest levels in which remains of ancient life have been found. It suggests that the Australopithecines did indeed create shelters no matter how rudimentary and makes viable the proposition that familial grouping of humankind was first developed by *Australopithecus*.

In perspective the life of the Australopithecine family and its possible larger manifestation, the troop, seems to have been that of a restricted wanderer. The evidence suggests that there were seasonal returns to favorite sites of lake and stream, indicating territorial ranges whose limits were known and observed. In this, *Australopithecus* was little different from other primates. There is no evidence for storage of foodstuffs, so that a day-by-day subsistence-seeking activity is manifest. In this, too, *Australopithecus* was no different from other primates. Where the great difference lies is in the presence of the permanent family group, the consistent making and use of tools, the creation of artificial shelter, and the great probability of language development along with growing intelligence. Such are the qualities hypothesized for *Australopithecus,* and in primate evolution, whatever the cause of their development, they are factors selective towards man.

The second of the three hominid groups is *Homo erectus.* *Homo erectus* appears to have been the dominant hominid form in the Old World a million years ago. In the 1930s its representatives, Java and Peking man, were celebrated as "missing links." In a sense this appellation still holds for *Homo erectus,* for the bipedalism, developing brain, familial habits, toolmaking, creation of shelter, and group habits established or hypothesized for *Australopithecus* are not only manifest but greatly developed in *Homo erectus.* It is generally admitted that *Homo erectus* is broadly ancestral to early forms of *Homo sapiens,* the third of the hominid groups. *Homo erectus* was taller and heavier than *Australopithecus,* and his head and brain were larger. He made tools and in the span of his terrestrial time seems to have innovated his toolmaking techniques so as to evolve the tools he used from simple pebbles flaked for cutting or cleaving purposes to bifacially flaked handaxes and sharp cutting and scraping tools made from flakes. *Homo erectus* could cook his food, live in caves or build shelters, and cooperate in such a fashion as to be able to corner and kill large mammals such as the elephant.

Recent discoveries seem to prove that *Homo erectus* had spread over the middle latitudes of the Old World from the borders of Manchuria to France. The site of Terra Amata is demonstrative of the evidence for present knowledge of the life and accomplishments of *Homo erectus.*

The Site

Along the Riviera, that warm and romantic Mediterranean coast which has been a playground of the rich and the not-so-rich in modern times, the remains of Paleolithic life are found in some abundance. From the maritime alpine background, freshwater streams have found their way to the warm sea across the short plains that intervene. Naturally rich in plant life, varied in the presence of numerous differing ecological niches, the region has always been attractive to animal life and thus to ancient men. Modern excavations in the city of Nice for commercial purposes revealed not only the tools and animal bones of ancient men but their hearths and huts as well. The commercial excavations were stopped, archaeologists took over, and the site turned out to be one of the most important Paleolithic discoveries of modern

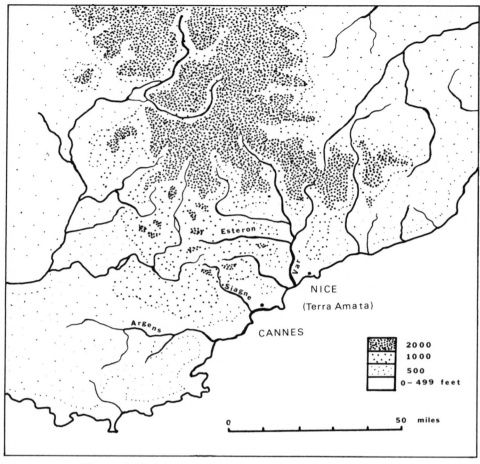

Nice and Vicinity

times. Called Terra Amata from the name of an alleyway nearby, the place was once a temporary site for ancient hunters who annually camped there in the late spring to take advantage of the amenities of the place.[1]

Some 300,000 years ago, towards the close of the third of Europe's great glacial stages—at a time when the sea was at least 50 feet higher than it is today and when the climate of the coast was colder though ameliorated by the sea—small groups of hunting-gathering people moved seasonally along traditional routes on the plain between sea and mountain. Not only were animals abundant but there were pebbles for the manufacture of stone tools at or near the beaches and good timber for wooden tools or other uses everywhere. The American geographer Carl O. Sauer has noted that seabeaches had advantages for early man that have to be considered in any review of the genesis of Paleolithic culture.[2] It is certain from the evidence furnished by sites such as Terra Amata that the beach, marine or otherwise, was one of the poles in the traditional yearly routes of the ancient men of this region and probably of many groups among the scattered and sparse populations of Afro-Eurasia. There are over fifty classes of seafood available at any given seabeach in temperate zones, many (such as plants and some of the invertebrates) leaving no trace to identify them archaeologically. Sufficient to note that the archaeologists have found evidence for the consumption of shellfish and fish at Terra Amata.

The group of ancient men represented at Terra Amata came to that campsite in the late spring or early summer presumably because it was a time of year when food-procuring opportunities were at their greatest. The young of large animals, such as the ibex, bear, wild ox, stag, and even elephant and rhino, were man's prey along with rodents, birds, and turtles. Among these animals, except perhaps the ibex, open parkland is an ideal environment, and in that environment these animals were difficult to hunt with ancient weapons. Presumably the shore of the small sea cove on which Terra Amata was situated was a point of concentration for such game. The fact that the young of the large animals were the principal food of the hunters probably means that it was the practice to kill only that which could be carried to the campsite and there quickly devoured, as the presence of meat at a camp is bound to attract predators.[3]

Of the twenty-one superimposed huts found at Terra Amata, ten were found in two groups on the ancient seabeach and eleven were located on a dune inland. All were of an elongated oval shape. Apparently the huts were built by thrusting long sticks (3 inches in diameter) in regular order into the ground. The closely placed stick walls were bent inward and attached in an unknown

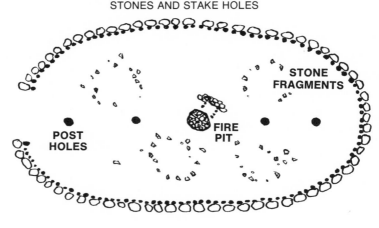

STONES AND STAKE HOLES

STONE
FRAGMENTS

POST
HOLES

FIRE
PIT

Terra Amata: plan of hut and artist's reconstruction.

fashion to substantial central stakes which ran down the middle of the structure. It is possible that there was a central ridge pole, but such evidence has not survived. In any case the hut was reinforced by placing stones around the outside at the base of the stick wall. Within, a hearth was situated towards the center of the room. This was either a shallow pit or a pebbled surface. Typically a line of stones was set on the northernmost side of the hearth, apparently as a windbreak—a mute comment perhaps on the draftiness of those most ancient houses.

In addition to sharpened animal bones, a few of which were found at Terra Amata, there were the inevitable stone tools. These were mostly core and pebble tools of types familiar to prehistorians because of their ubiquity in the sites of the Old World Early Paleolithic. The excavators found that the stone tool industry associated with the beach huts was dominated by the cruder pebble tools and that the industry of the sand-dune huts, while including tool types found in the beach huts, also included more advanced tools, some of which were made on flakes. The differences between the industries were probably due to special activities carried out in each place. The flake tool types resemble the well-known Clactonian industries of Western Europe and the core and pebble tools of both groups of huts belong to the Early Acheulean, one of Western Europe's earliest toolmaking traditions. Within the huts it was possible to discern areas where, according to the excavator, one or another of the occupants had sat while making tools out of beach pebbles. The worker is presumed to have sat on animal skins surrounded by the flinty debris created by his efforts.

Except for the possibility that an enigmatic imprint in the sand, spherical in shape and filled with some white stuff, was a wooden bowl or dish, and the presence of some sticks of red ocher, there is little evidence from which to build a complete picture of this most ancient way of life—yet prehistorians count themselves fortunate to have so much.

No human remains were found. A footprint was discerned, however, and its measurement, 9½ inches, was used as a means of

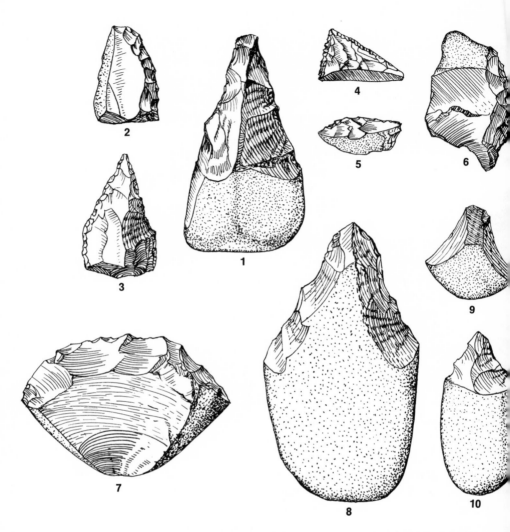

Stone tools at Terra Amata. 1: hand ax; 2, 3, 4, 5, 6: cutting and scraping tools made on flakes; 7, 8, 9, 10: pebble tools.

defining an individual perhaps 5 feet 1 inch in height. By age and by the association of the stone industries elsewhere it is probable that the people of Terra Amata were of *Homo erectus* type. Some prehistorians would also place them with Neanderthal man, the most famous of the fossil men of the Old World, and thus representative of *Homo sapiens* in the early Paleolithic.

Pollen analysis of fossilized human feces found among the huts provides evidence for the late spring or early summer arrival time; stratigraphic evidence suggests that each visit was of very short duration and that the huts were temporary, collapsing after each visit. Precise superimposition of hut floor upon hut floor indicates that the same people returned year after year.

The huts were sizable, ranging from 26 feet to 49 feet long and from 13 feet to about 20 feet in width. They were obviously built to hold a number larger than the ordinary family of father, mother, and several children. This raises an important question as to the social character of the Terra Amata group. It is obvious that the construction of a shelter large enough to hold several families reflects a social organization more complex than any one of those families. One could of course argue that the ancient family was of the extended type—that is, that all the brothers' or sisters' families resided together—but this kind of residence group has really little to distinguish it from the lowest level of social organization which anthropologists define: the band. At this distance in time and with the limitations of the material evidence, there is little basis upon which to make such a distinction. However, there are more than faint clues as to that ancient life and how it was organized.

Life in the Primitive Band

Anthropologists have been fortunate in that, in spite of the ravages of Western man, a few primitive people survived intact far enough into the nineteenth and twentieth centuries for their cultures to be recorded before extinction. Among these people, the Philippine Negritos, the Andaman Islanders, the Semang of the Malay Peninsula, the Pygmies of the Congo, the Bushmen of both South Africa and Australia, the Ona and the Yahgan of Tierra del Fuego, the Eskimo, and some others have been lumped together as representatives of the band. Bands are made up of hunters and gatherers and accordingly are nomadic. Each band consists of twenty-five to sixty people, who tend to have few material possessions. Because of the need to forage widely, bands tend to scatter over the landscape, observing territorial limits so that each band has its own share of the subsistence productivity. Reasonably fixed routes are taken within these territories, depending on seasonal changes. Relations within and between bands are typically those of marriage, though cooperation in other affairs may occur.

Each band is made up of nuclear families, bound together by an intimacy which approaches that of the family itself. Indeed the nuclear family has often less importance to the individual than the band of which he is a member. One of the characteristics that distinguish man from the other primates is the observance of incest taboos, and it is often cultural norms that determine how far these taboos extend above and beyond the nuclear family. The band is a case in point, as marriage rules seem to have been based chiefly on incest taboos.

Bands are egalitarian, and part of their cohesiveness comes from the leadership contributed by individual members according to the needs of a given situation. This fluidity of leadership has a strong selective value. One critical development in man's rise to civilization is the increasing rigidity of leadership brought on by institutionalization. One man or one group of men cannot have answers for each and every crisis in human affairs. A society that can develop leadership as needed has a better chance of survival than one that depends on the genius of a single man—as history often tragically demonstrates.

Men and women are generally equals in band life. Men forage widely in search of game. Women, because they must care for the children and maintain the campsite, forage nearby. Men cooperate in hunting because group action is an advantage both in killing game and in bringing it home. Since the labor of the women—such as the obtainment of vegetable foods—does not often require cooperation, there is a somewhat differing world view between the sexes because of different economic tasks.

At the heart of the cohesiveness of the band is the sense of mutuality. Food sharing is essential, and no one in a group in which all are dependent must be without his or her share of the subsistence. This has its expression in the sense of obligation of each member of the band to every other. This obligation goes far beyond the simple sharing of food and extends to childrearing, storytelling, and common possession.

The world of the band member is one which makes little distinction between that which can be comprehended because it can be seen, touched, heard, or smelled and that which is known because it must be. A thing to exist has to have a spirit, whether one means a flower, an animal, a stone, or a man. Death is the absence of spirit. The band exists because it has a spirit above and beyond the life of any individual, and this may be given ritual form in a totem, a representation in graphic though not necessarily material form of that spirit. It is an acknowledgment of the essential spirit quality of the world that man observes rites of passage symbolizing the individual's growth, maturity, and death. The observance of such rituals establishes identity not only of individual members but of the band itself, as each band has its own identifying rituals.

Bands and the People of Terra Amata

Among the stones identified at Terra Amata was one of volcanic origin which could only come from the region of Estérel, southwest of Cannes, a little over 30 miles from Nice. That and the evidence for temporary and brief but repeated seasonal stay at Terra Amata suggests that the hunters moved over territorial ranges of large but reasonably limited extent. Within these foraging territories were established routes leading to good campgrounds where there was fresh water and, according to season, abundance of certain foodstuffs.

At the campsite, temporary shelters were built, one or two being sufficient to shelter the whole group at any one time. Considerable doubt has been cast on the interpretation of the excavators that stone debris found in the huts is the waste of toolmaking. On the beaches and dunes, the most important function of the houses was to shelter both people and food supplies from the wind. The single hearth in each hut suggests that interior fires were for cooking or light rather than warmth. The line of stones on the northwest of each hearth may well be an additional windbreak, indicating that fire may have been difficult to obtain (no fire-making tools have been preserved). It is more likely, however, that the line of stones represents a traditional structure used in cooking. It seems evident that the huts were used as cooking and sleeping places—the skin mat reputed to mark the stoneworker's sitting place could equally well be interpreted as bedding. It is hard to see living space fractionalized by stone workers when such activity could be better performed outside. The preparation of stones for use in the hut proper is more in line with the existential quality of the primitive world.

It should be noted that complete tools are found in some abundance amid the living floors of Paleolithic camps. This comports with the nomadic quality of band life. Stones are, after all, heavy—but tools can be made from them easily. An hour or two of work with beach pebbles provided what tools were needed. It is probable that tools were left each year in situ—along with other possessions, as the "wooden bowl" suggests—to be used again on return. It is typical of band groups to cache tools at seasonal camps so as not to have to carry them about. Wood and bone weapons and tools are lighter and sharper than those of stone and were probably carried about more commonly than the stone axes and choppers which have given a label to prehistoric man. The small number of bone tools found at Terra Amata may well be owing to their portability and greater use as much as to the accident of preservation. Furthermore the stone tools recovered are largely for purposes of chopping, scraping, pounding, and cutting—all processes used more in the preparation of food than in its obtainment.

The technology of bands is simple and tends to fall into two main categories: tools used in hunting and gathering—such as weapons, digging sticks, canoes, traps, carrying baskets, and nets—and tools used in the preparation of food—such as pots, pounders, and cutting and piercing devices. Although there is some overlap in these categories, they are often distinguished by portability. It is more than likely, then, that the stone tools of Early Paleolithic man were primarily for food preparation, for which their function and weight were assets.

If then one can argue for a pattern of nomadism commensurate with that known for modern primitive bands, does it follow that the people of Terra Amata exhibited the other elements, material and immaterial, that make up bands? The answer depends on two factors, the first being the acceptance of the people of Terra Amata as men distinguished from other primates by the ability to make tools, to build shelters and fires, to observe incest taboos and thus to preserve the customs of social life regarding the human relationships of parents and children, male and female while continuing the species; the second being the acceptance of the nomadism evidenced at Terra Amata as indicating the type of social behavior known to anthropologists as familial. Here the size of the Terra Amata shelters evidences more than the simple family. As to the first factor, the evidence is overwhelming that it is truly man— primeval as he may be—to which Terra Amata bears witness. As to the second, the archaeological evidence is as secure as we can ever expect for so remote a time. In the light of this evidence, the characteristics of known bands can by analogy—and with all due caution—be applied to the men of Terra Amata.

One other faint and tantalizing hint of the character of past life is there. The red ocher sticks, known by their wear to have been used, evidence color usage—perhaps, as the excavators suggest, for body painting. Red ocher, however, can also be material for drawing and painting. Since art is communication functional in its universality as a means of describing and thus controlling the supernatural, the red ocher is an important clue. The word *art,* however, unlocks a Pandora's box. There is a quality of mystery in the purposeful use of coloring or line drawing. If a man paints a red blotch on his forehead, he is not quite the same as he was before he was painted. He is now the object of laughter, pride, scorn, or puzzlement. He is different, no matter how slightly, from what he was previously, and the degree of reaction to him by his peers depends on the extent of his change. Circles, squares, squiggles, are symbols, not doodles, in the mind of primitive man. If the man calls his circle ''rabbit'' and the others recognize it as such, it is almost the same as holding a rabbit before the group. What is conveyed by the symbol is not a rabbit but the *idea* of *rabbit,* which can be repeated again and again. It is this ability to use graphic or oral symbols consistently to convey ideas that distinguishes man. Are our humble red ocher sticks the evidence for the conveyance of ideas through symbols no matter how simple? The fact of the matter is that the presence of red ocher means red color was desired.

Whereas all primitive people distinguish light and dark, black and white, they often refer to other colors by analogy: mouse-colored (gray), sky-colored (blue), fire-colored (red).[4] Red is the next color referred to by name after black and white in the evolution of primitive languages. However people at Terra Amata vocalized black and white, the presence of red ocher unquestionably indicates that their vocal vocabulary gave that ocher a name —perhaps *sticklike.* The naming of color without reference to things is to name an abstraction. For primitive man such abstractions are difficult, if not impossible, for what is green or orange is seen to be so only in reference to the phenomena with which such colors occur. A similar statement could be made for sound, smell, and touch.

The number of tools in the Terra Amata hut, the shelters, the different animals and plants recounted yearly, the seasonal changes, the specificity of designating human relations and relationships, the routes marked by tradition, the extraterritorial bands, the rites of passage that marked the individual life cycle, the use of color and a variety of materials are motivational factors in the expansion of spoken vocabulary. Language is another cohesive force in the life of the group, and there seems little doubt that our scraps of evidence are witness to its presence on a plane many degrees

above the innate utterances and facial grimaces of primate ancestors.

Terra Amata in Prehistory

Terra Amata is rare and indeed almost unique in the evidence it
offers for the life of so remote a time in human history. But prehistorians are familiar with the tools and weapons found at Terra
Amata, because they are of the type found widely in much of the
Old World—demonstrating that the way of life at Terra Amata was
to be found wherever men searched for subsistence. Two hundred
thousand or more years were to elapse before the life style indicated
at Terra Amata would evolve to something else (Table 2, Appendix).
Why did it not change sooner? The answer must be that the cultural
values of this band system of society were so elastic and sensitive to
human needs that there were no reasons for permanent change even
though innovations doubtless occurred from time to time.

What then was the anomaly in this paradigm of ancient existence? More than likely it was the effect of optimum hunting and
gathering conditions which permitted longer stays at one place and
caused concentrations of bands and smaller groups in immediately
contiguous if not in aggregate circumstances. Greater population
and the intensification of human relations strain traditional forms
of social organization and behavior as local social values are challenged by extralocal ones. As long as people can move away from
one another, indigenous values will be preserved. When diverse
people concentrate together, there are challenges to those values in
everything from social reciprocity to individual prowess. Perhaps
the spread of generally similar tool types throughout the Old
World was due to a natural tendency to avoid challenges to one's
society. Paradoxically, exogamous practices required social exchanges so that no group desired to move into absolute isolation.
Perhaps the preservation of social distance was as instrumental in
moving man across geographical space as was the availability of

game. The anomaly then was the inability of otherwise excellently adapted bands of mankind to create a social organization which would permit greater aggregations to live in harmony. The attractions of optimum hunting and gathering conditions could be diminished by this inability. Aggression was to be avoided. One's way of life was to be preserved even at the cost of movement away from the best areas. So long as there was space for such movement, and there was in much of the Pleistocene period, the small populations which made up the bands were preserved. But a time came when such movement was no longer possible and a new paradigm was created out of ancient anomaly.

Cognition Stage

In the context of cognition growth, the immediacy of the relationship between man and his physical and social environment at Terra Amata is significant. Physical survival depended on an animal awareness of prey, of the sites of food, of route, of predator danger and defense, of seasonal advantages and disadvantages. Social survival depended on a human understanding of place within the group relative to sex, leadership, age, and physical capability. Relationship on the basis of consanguinity or nonconsanguinity was distinguished in the practice of exogamy—a manifestation of ikonic behavior—but social cohesiveness depended mainly on an enactive mutuality because of the demands of the nuclear family and its extension to the other members of the band. Tactility and the gesture were dominant physical acts of communication but oral language enhanced communication, and one can presume that both image creation and a degree of symbolism were involved in ancient Terra Amata speech.

As to world view it is suggested that it was largely dependent on that which was immediate in both the environment and consequent experience. Consciousness of that which was mysterious in the spirit of things is possibly implied both by the presence of coloring matter and the analogy to modern band systems, both of which indicate an ikonic perception.

The cognitive level of the people represented at Terra Amata was thus largely enactive but in language, religion, and related world view, as well as in social organization, another and higher level of awareness is suggested. Rudimentary as it probably was, it nonetheless was a step in the evolution of culture toward civilization.

5

Dolni

Vestonice

The Appearance of *Homo sapiens*

A QUARTER OF A MILLION YEARS had passed since the band of Terra Amata had had its day. Europe had been subject to a massive glaciation and a long warm interglacial onset which ended with a new ice advance: the great Würm glaciation. This was the last of the glacial stages which dramatized the Pleistocene. It was to endure around one hundred thousand years, years in which there would be ice advances and retreats which made the unglaciated lands colder or warmer according to these fluctuations. Some of these lands are found in a broad belt skirting the mountains of Europe and reaching far from France and Southern Germany to the Ukraine and beyond into Central Asia. South of this belt, along the shores of the warm Mediterranean, the low sea level exposed long connected stretches of land and provided a nursing ground for man, plants, and animals alike. With sea level rise at the end of the Pleistocene, this ancient breeding ground was submerged and its history largely lost to the present, but north in Central Europe a similar breeding ground flourished in spite of exigency.

Man had by now become *Homo sapiens,* man the wise, the an-

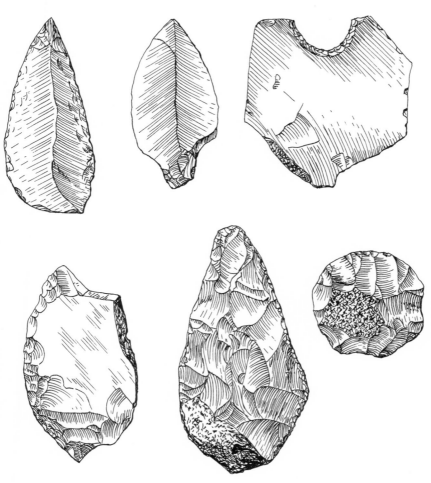

Mousterian stone tools. Most Mousterian tools were made out of flakes and were manufactured for purposes of scraping, cutting, and puncturing. Core tools, however, were also made to add to the hunter-gatherers' technological repertoire. The core tools shown here are from the repertoire usually associated with Neanderthal man.

cestor of modern man. The evidence is that modern man (*Homo sapiens sapiens*) had perhaps evolved through a stage resembling that of *Homo erectus,* with a larger brain capacity, greater stature, and a more sophisticated cultural form with which are associated such artifacts as the Mousterian stone industries. This stage of hominid development is encompassed in the name Neanderthal.

Neanderthal men were short, powerful creatures with a cranial capacity as large as modern man's. Rugged in appearance owing to massive brow ridges, a low forehead, large teeth, and chinlessness, their primitive look was belied by a belief in the supernatural as evidenced by deliberate burials, often with "grave furniture." Neanderthals lived in caves, rock shelters, and presumably in tents or lean-tos. Their terrestrial life began towards the end of the third interglacial stage, perhaps two hundred thousand or more years ago, and ended sometime in the midst of the last glaciation, at least in Europe when truly modern men were in the ascent.

The *Homo sapiens* of modern type was widespread in the late Pleistocene but seems to have achieved a kind of cultural climax in Western and Central Europe. For it was he who created the famous cave paintings and little sculptures, as well as the achievement of the most sophisticated technological level of the Old Stone Age. It is this primeval cultural climax of the late Pleistocene that provides a vivid insight into a critical step in man's evolvement towards civilization. The site of Dolni Vestonice in Central Europe, because of the remarkable preservation of remains more than 25,000 years old, provides a magnificent case study of this step.

The Site

Out of the ancient mountains that formed the boundary of the old kingdoms of Bohemia and Moravia, that now shape the central portion of the modern state of Czechoslovakia, there flow a series of streams and rivers trending east and south. Moravia is mountainous and hilly, but in the vicinity of Brünn, the second city of Moravia, the valleys are broader and the gradient less. It is a fertile region rich in agricultural produce. In the vicinity of Brünn a number of the principal streams join and flow southward through gentler, loessic, fertile lands until the mainstream encounters the limestone barrier of the Pollau Mountains. Here the waters are augmented by several tributary rivers, among them the Thaya, the southernmost stream of Moravia. This accumulation of waters in the gentle valley in front of the Pollau creates a marshy situation

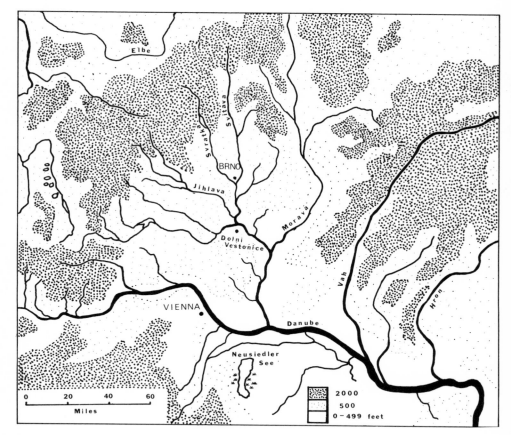

Central Europe

out of which the mainstream meanders eastward, then south, until it joins the March River which marks the boundary with Hungary. Eventually the March, after flowing across a great plain, joins the Danube at Pressberg where that historic river breaks through the Little Carpathian Mountains and enters the plains of Hungary.

Emphasis has to be placed on this geography, for the whole region has produced abundant archaeological evidence that in the Upper Paleolithic it was an area of great attraction for ancient man. The Pollau hills on the south of the Thaya Valley can be called an outrider of the Alps, while just to the north, forming the other wall of the valley, begin the Carpathian ranges which separate Central Europe from the plains of Poland and Russia. The gap between creates a gateway: to the west the hilly country of Bohe-

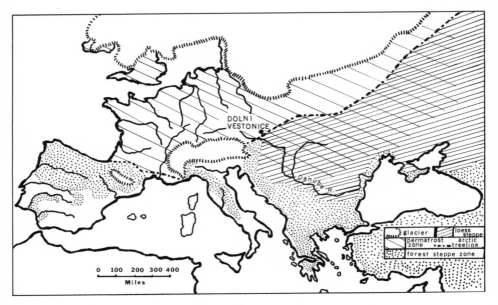

Location of Ice in Würm Times

mia and the marshlands of Austria, to the southeast the plains of
Hungary. It is this precisely defined and varied geographical situation which, with the marshland and riverine ecological regimes,
provided the basis for successful settlement for man even amid the
glacially motivated climatic changes of the late Pleistocene.

On the northward-facing hillslopes of the Pollau, hunting-
gathering groups in some number made their settlements, sometime in the period between 29,000 and 25,000 years ago, at the
beginning of a third phase of the great fourth glaciation of Europe,
that of Würm. Southern Moravia and the lower regions south, as
well as much of the Danube Valley, were unglaciated but were
subject to the extremes of cold brought about by the presence of
the great ice sheets on the north and the glaciers of the mountains
northeast and west. The climate was arctic, with long winters and
short summers. The biota was of taiga-tundra type: in the more
protected valleys conifers, willow, and other flora flourished,
while in the open plains tundra-steppe life marked the summer
seasons. Fauna included mammoths, rhino, fox, wolf, cave bear,
reindeer, cave lion, wolverines, bison, hares, and the lynx—all apparently of arctic type.[1]

The settlement of Dolni Vestonice was strategically situated on a slope next to a small stream that ran with some rapidity from the Pollau slopes above the settlement into the marshy land of the Thaya Valley. The hard ground of the slope extended into the marshlands as a spur. Thus on the lower part of the settlement there was a natural barrier on three sides. This part of the site was occupied, it appears, earlier than the upper portion. It is the upper section—bounded by marshlands only on the side where the stream debouched—which has provided wonderful evidence for ancient life.

The upper settlement of Dolni Vestonice is situated on soliflucted ground which has caused some disturbance of the original layout of the place. What is revealed, however, is a settlement which had been occupied from time to time with some regularity over an extended period. One of the latest occupations is presumed to be one of the most extensive. It certainly is the best preserved.

The excavations were begun before World War II and regularly continued after that time. The German burning in 1945 of a nearby chateau where much of the excavated material of the prewar years was stored helped to motivate renewed excavation.

The settlement plan consisted of at least four huts located erratically within a walled compound and a hut outside the compound farther up the slope. Most apparent at the site was the accumulation of mammoth bones in separate piles near the huts and in an extended heap, particularly on both banks and in the midst of the stream basin. Most of the mammoths were young ones; one pile of bones is estimated to represent over one hundred such animals. Stone "butchering" tools were found in association with some of the mammoth remains. Tusks and other massive bone of the mammoth were found, some stuck into the ground, and are the essential stuff of the main compound wall and other slighter walls. The massing of bones as a part of walls is assumed by the excavators, but stone was also used. The upright tusks and bones were probably used to spread skins here and there as a part of the barrier.

The huts are generally ovoid and usually contain a number of

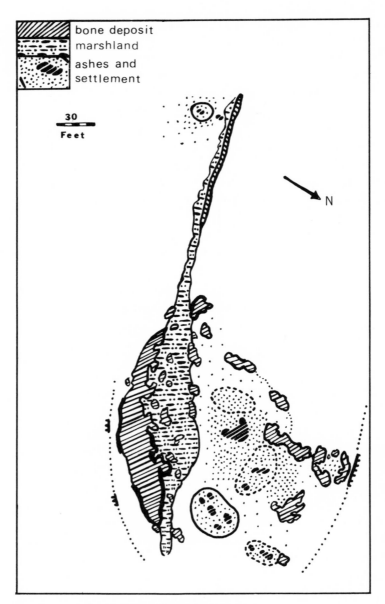

bone deposit

marshland

ashes and
settlement

30
Feet

N

The Upper Settlement of Dolni Vestonice

hearths. The one exception is a hut located near a large, centrally located, outside hearth.

As determined by the excavation, the huts were built of upright posts inclined inward but probably not meeting, or at any rate leaving room for a smoke hole. The hut or tent frame was covered with skins—probably of the mammoth—and the uprights supported by heavy stones. These were not small structures: the largest measured 27 by 45 feet and had five hearths within. Some experts say this one was unroofed, though both wood and the large skins of the mammoth were available for roofing. The ovoid shape of all these structures strongly suggests an effort to reduce the area which had to be roofed while permitting the double reinforcement brought about by the joining of walls tent-fashion.

Within the huts was the accumulation of daily life, stone, bone, ivory, and clay artifacts, hearth remains, and enigmatic bits and pieces of material which by association, type, and distribution evidence able, efficient, and effective survival of the inhabitants.

The Artifacts

The stone (basically flint) industry is a familiar one to the archaeologists of Europe. It is referred to as the Gravettian, or rather the Eastern Gravettian, though Bohuslav Klima, the excavator of Dolni Vestonice, prefers to refer to it as the Pollauan because of certain local characteristics. Essentially the Gravettian is of the blade tool industries of the Upper Paleolithic: it consists of several kinds of scrapers, burins or engraving tools, knives, points—some of which are shouldered, suggesting missile points, denticulated blades, awls and drills, and chisels. There are also sickle and saw blades. Basically, the industry is diminutive and suggests that hafting in lengths of bone and wood was commonplace. Larger stones were used for the various purposes for which heft and weight were necessary. In the Gravettian industry can be identified the processes of cutting, piercing, scraping, chopping, smashing, shaving, and carving, useful to the hunter and his wife

Reconstruction of settlement at Dolni Vestonice.

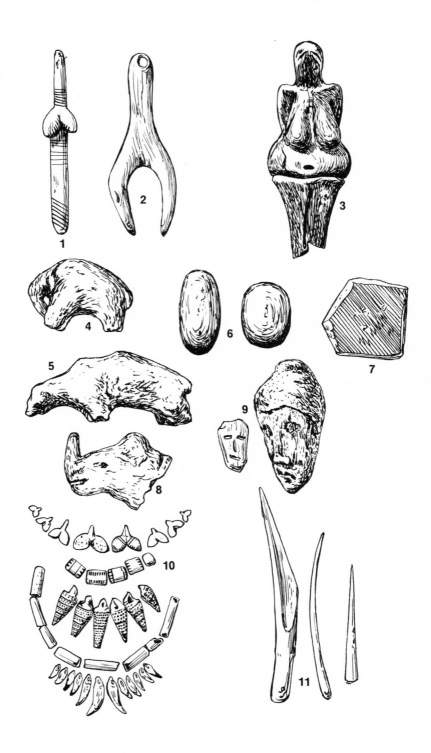

(*Left*) Artifacts found at Dolni Vestonice. 1, 2: stylized figurines in bone; 3: female figurine in clay; 4, 5: animal figurines in clay; 6: ground stones; 7: ground stone palette; 8: figurine of a rhinoceros in clay; 9: carvings of deformed faces; 10: necklace beads of clay, bone, shell, and teeth; 11: bone needles or punches.

whether dealing with the flesh and bone of animals, the stuff of plants, or the versatilities of wood. There are some rounded and smoothed pebbles and plates of stone used for or created by rubbing or grinding. This plus the presence of the denticulated blades—which are similar to the sickle blades of a much later period of food gathering (see chapter 6)—suggests that these ancient people were well aware of the values of local plant life and may well have harvested it seasonally, perhaps grinding seeds for food, and leaves, bark, and stems for coloring matter. Whatever the actual fact, the Gravettian industry is a sophisticated one, almost peerless in the history of the Paleolithic generally. It gave ancient men an adaptive capability which unquestionably made possible the wide-ranging settlement of the times. The Gravettian industrial tradition, whatever its origins, is spread from France to the Soviet Ukraine—a tribute to its applicability to local situations. Although other earlier artifact traditions of the Paleolithic—such as the Abbevillian, Acheulean, and Mousterian—are spread geographically even farther, the complexities of the Gravettian with its specific tool usages is in marked contrast to the generalized tools of those earlier industries.

The bone and ivory artifacts, while nowhere as numerous as those of stone, still add a significant dimension to the Gravettian tool repertoire. Included are bone points, spatulas or smoothing sticks, needles and awls, grooved rubbers, lance heads, knives, shovel-like antler plates, and bone tubes. Fossilized shells and freshwater molluscs, coupled with ivory and bone pendants, tubes, and other pierced materials were used as beads in necklaces.

A Unique Hut and a Burial

Up the slope about 250 feet from the walled settlement and across the stream, a circular, semisubterranean hut was discovered. The semisubterranean quality was caused by excavation into

Burial of a woman at Dolni Vestonice.

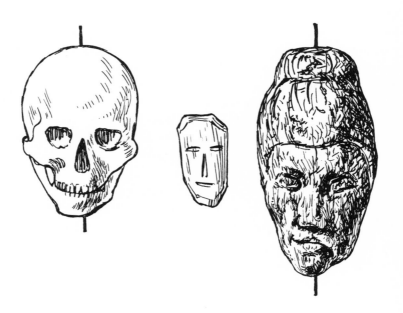

Distorted face of the woman of Dolni Vestonice. The skull at the left is an artist's projection based on the ivory tablet (*center*) and mammoth-ivory head found at Dolni Vestonice.

the slope. A limestone retaining wall held the posts of the roof. The whole hut is some 18 feet in diameter. At its center was a clay oven (earth and pulverized limestone) within which were found over two thousand clay pieces, none of which appear to be the debris of daily activity. Most are shapeless, but some represent the heads, feet, and bodies of animals. A few hollow long bones found in the hut have been identified as probably flutes or pipes. All the evidence indicated that this hut housed a special activity of the settlement; additional evidence appeared in 1949, with the finding of the skeleton of a female buried in a pit within the living compound. The body lay on its right side in a contracted position and was concealed by two mammoth scapulae. The use of mammoth bones for that purpose is well evidenced in the Upper Paleolithic of Europe. Bones and teeth of an arctic fox were found near the hand of the deceased as if she had held the carcass when buried. By her head was a flint point. Her hand and chest were covered with red ocher—again a common burial practice of the time. When the badly damaged skull was repaired, it was revealed that the smallish female had had a pathological condition which had caused paralysis of the cheek muscles of the left side of the face. In other words, an obvious physical deformation had helped set the individual apart from the others of the settlement, and this was presumably involved in the reason why she had been buried in this special way.

This special quality was underlined by the knowledge of the discovery in the living portion of the site in 1936 of a sculptured head of a woman in ivory and in 1948 of a woman's face carved on a small ivory tablet. In both these cases there is obvious distortion of the left portion of the face.

One of the famous "Venus figurines" found at Upper Paleolithic sites from France to the Ukraine was found in the open fireplace of the settlement. It was made of fired clay mixed with pulverized bone, and emphasized the breasts, hips, and pregnancy of the female while face and extremities were minimized.

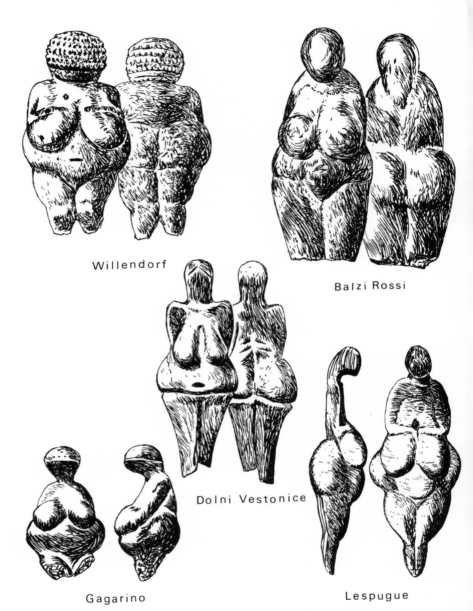

Willendorf

Balzi Rossi

Dolni Vestonice

Gagarino

Lespugue

Gravettian "Venuses."

The Climate and the Land

The analysis of the soil and pollen evidence at Dolni Vestonice, though incomplete, strongly suggests that though the climate at the time of the upper settlement was of arctic type, it was not as extreme as one might expect. The evidence indicates that ancient Dolni Vestonice began in a period when the climate was almost temperate and was abandoned when the climate became increasingly colder and drier. The river valleys and much of the surrounding region were in a life zone of taiga type for much of that time, while the open plains to the east and south were under near tundra conditions. Spruce, pine, larch, juniper, the European elm, and the fir have been identified, and with these trees it can be assumed that dry-land grasses and various marshland flora were present. Some of these grasses have been identified by pollen analysis, but their association with the site is uncertain. Broadleaf trees were found along the riverbanks or wherever water was abundant. Furthermore, it can also be assumed that as the climate became more frigid the taiga biota shrank.

Thus it is possible to define at least three life zones at the time of Dolni Vestonice's maximum settlement: (1) the taiga-forested low hills and valleys extending into the open plains dominated by conifers, (2) the tundra-steppe plains which in summer are presumed to have been covered with northern grasses, and (3) the swamp lands and river valleys. The rivers in the region are today in stages of maturity, and a similar situation can be presumed in the past. On the edges of the swamps and along the riverbanks grew grasses, reeds, and broadleaf trees, such as the elm and probably the beech, birch, and alder.

The site of Dolni Vestonice is situated on a tongue of the first zone which protrudes into the third. The inhabitants were thus able to take advantage of the flora of the swamp and had there also a supply of molluscs and fish but would in summer have been plagued with the flies that swampland nurtures.

Mammoths and Men

The evidence for extensive subsistence dependence on the mammoth and particularly the mammoth young has a direct bearing upon the time of year in which the settlement was occupied. Though the habits of the mammoth cannot be observed directly, there is considerable paleontological information available, primarily because the soft parts of the body are known on account of their preservation in the frozen soils of Siberia and Alaska. Henry Fairfield Osborn, the American paleontologist whose monumental work *Probiscidia* is the definitive study of fossil elephants, has the following to say about the mammoth:

> It proves that the extremely hypsodont, finely plated teeth of the mammoth are principally adapted to the northern grasses which prevail on the tundras and Arctic prairies during the summer season. As recently described by Stefansson, the summer tundra flora closely imitates that of the grasslands which we know as "prairies" in temperate latitudes. In this brief season the mammoth obtained its chief food supply for the year, and, like other northern Herbivora, stored up large reservoirs of fat which were drawn upon during the long Arctic winter season. In summer a grazer chiefly if not exclusively, in winter it became a browser, feeding upon twigs and the branches of conifers and woody substances which contained materials of far less nutritional value. Thus its habits directly reversed those of the African elephant (*Loxodonta*), which is chiefly a browser and incidentally, and for the sake of food variety, a grazer, or of the Indian elephant, which is both a browser and a grazer. Similar seasonal habits are doubtless characteristic of the northern types of horses with extremely hypsodont teeth primarily adapted to grazing, secondarily to browsing.[2]

The importance of this conclusion of Osborn's is obvious. If the three-life-zone determination of the ancient environment has validity, the habits of the mammoth were seasonally keyed to those zones. Though much has to be learned about the behavioral pattern of modern elephants, which are still relatively unknown for all the publicity associated with elephants, it is clear that the individual elephant has quantitatively an immense subsistence requirement. A mature elephant requires 400 to 600 pounds of foodstuffs per day. In a sampling of 71 African elephants, it was discovered that 87 percent of their total food intake was grass and around 10 percent leaves, twigs, and bark.[3] Osborn's statement emphasizes the tundra flora as in effect a replacement grassland. Accordingly, the mammoths of Moravia must have sought the second of the life zones *in summer* when the flora of that zone had its most abundant growth. As the short summer ended, the animals gravitated back to the first zone.

At one time African elephants characteristically migrated over vast distances, thus ensuring the finding of adequate shade, nutritional variety, salt and water supplies. In addition, the opportunity was provided for herd regrouping and large congregations, numbering up to 100 animals or more, were sometimes formed. These migrations were of two types: localised wet-season meanderings and long-distance, directional migrations covering several hundred miles per annum. In different seasons, elephants invariably seek certain localities— open country during the rains, and forest in the dry season. Thus, on Kilimanjaro, elephants move down the northern slopes of the Usambara range about April and spread out through the Nyika plains almost to the coast. The wanderings of elephants in other parts of East Africa are likewise governed by the availability of food.[4]

As the grass of the tundra region became unobtainable because of snowfall and ice, so the mammoth's food resource was changed to the trees whose bark, twigs, and leaves then became the supplement to the fat supply created in the individual by the summer abundance. Plant growth at the edge of the swamps and along the riverbanks caused concentrations of mammoths into the third zone during the height of the winter. The mammoth's winter months were thus the equivalent of the elephant's dry season. In other words, the mammoth wintered precisely in the area where the people of Dolni Vestonice were settled.[5]

Studies of African elephants show no special breeding time. On an annual increase of about 7 percent there were no peaks to indicate a specific breeding season.[6] African elephants tend to break up into family units of from five to a dozen or more, and within these groups the young and the sexes seek each other's company.[7] At the time of major seasonal migration to other areas elephants congregate and move in large herds, apparently as a protective measure. Aggregation in a feeding ground is thus familial and grouped according to maturity and sex.

As noted by the British mammalogist D. F. Vesey-Fitzgerald, "During the rains the herds tend to disperse. Water and green grass become available over a wide area and the animals are not only protected by the spaciousness of their territory, but by the fact that they are more difficult to encounter in it."[8] It is in the dry season, when the animals concentrate, that they are most vulnerable, and in view of the young's concentration within the larger concentration they are particularly vulnerable. The mammoths' aggregation in the winter months appears to have been similar to the African elephants' dry season aggregation and thus had the same vulnerability to the hunter. (There is evidence that over a thousand mammoths, young and adult, were slaughtered by hunters living in the large Gravettian site of Predmosti some 50 miles northeast of Dolni Vestonice.)

On the basis of the evidence, then, Dolni Vestonice and other Gravettian camps of Central Europe on which the mammoth depended for at least part of the year were winter camps.

It is clear from the number of young mammoths found at Dolni Vestonice that not only were the hunters selective in their kills but that the kills were made in the vicinity of the settlement. All parts of the young mammoths are found in the deposits, indicating that the whole animal was brought to the site for butchering—a task of some magnitude. (Young African elephants—1 to 10 years old— can weigh from 200 to 3,000 pounds.) The accumulation of meat on the site must have been considerable, and in summer the flies and the rapid deterioration of the meat have to be considered as negative evidence for the existence of a settlement at Dolni Vestonice at that season of the year. Furthermore, predators would have been drawn to the vulnerable camp by meat accumulation. In winter, however, the icy conditions would have preserved meat and moderated the predator-drawing odors.

The Ancient Diet

Obviously the people of Dolni Vestonice supplemented their diet with other foodstuff than that of mammoths. Hare and foxes accounted for 17 to 25 percent of the fauna identified, and reindeer and wolf totaled 11 percent. The mammoth comprised 25 percent. All other animals were below these in quantity. Foxes and wolves were probably killed for their pelts; the reindeer, the horse, the bison, and the hare provided food as well as other animal products. The amount of plant food consumed is unknown but its importance as a major food resource is indicated by the possible presence of hazelnuts and the known availability of such edible plants or plant products as arctic berries, the water nut (*Trapanatans*), the bog bean (*Menyanthes trifoliata*), the common reed (*Phragmites communis*), and the wild cereal grass (*Glyceria fluitans*)—all of which are common to the marshy zones of Northern Europe—plus the presence of sickle blades and grinding stones. It is notable too that well into the last century pine and birch bark were used as food supplements in Europe.[9] Most of these plant products were ground and the resulting meal used in various ways by European peasants for whose activities there is a record.

The dietary habits of ancient man have been studied only in the grossest fashion. It appears that life expectancy for the Pollauan individual was probably no more than twenty or twenty-five years and always slightly less for the women, for whom the problems of childbearing were apparently often fatal in one way or another. At the Gravettian site of Predmosti a grave was found containing the bodies of twelve children and eight adults. This is evidence perhaps for a high death rate, which would normally be characterized by high child mortality. There is little question that natural selection weeded out the unfit and insured the survival of healthy and vigorous individuals. Environmental stress, the disease vectors for settlements in marshlands, the constant state of vigilance and activity, and the tensions of cultural participation have to be added to the dangers of living in the Pleistocene world, where predators flourished, the whole adding up to a short but vigorous lifespan. Caloric intake was probably quite high since animal products have a high calorie count.[10] Man by this time had had several hundreds of thousands of years of experience in learning to balance his diet pragmatically. For the people of Dolni Vestonice settlement in winter next to or partially within a marshland had subsistence advantage. The site was also protected from the worst part of the arctic storms by the surrounding mountains and hills, and the ameliorating effects of the warmer swamps and waters made life a little easier.

Yet when the winter ended and the flies returned to the marshes, men and animals (like the Eskimo and animals of the north) moved onto the plains. On the plains the abundant flora drew the ungulates in their herds, and this plus the presence of berries and other edible plants drew men far from the winter settlement. Whereas concentration of human settlement had advantage in winter, summer dispersal of animal herds made similar dispersal necessary for man.

Clues to Social Organization

The pattern of summer dispersal and winter concentration, which the habits of mammals such as the mammoth suggest, provides clues for the probable character of the social organization of the people of Dolni Vestonice—and probably for the Gravettian groups of Central Europe as a whole. It is clear that the winter camp was composed of at least four identical living units, number-ing in each case from 20 to 25 or more individuals. This is evi-denced by the size and number of the huts and their hearths. In all, then, the camp consisted of 80 to 125 persons. That it was a delib-erate aggregation of people having several cultural themes in com-mon is evidenced by the wall with which they surrounded them-selves, by hut proximity, and by artifact repertoire. The hunting of mammoths required the cooperation of many if not all of the male members of the group. Karl Absolon, the original excavator at Dolni Vestonice, found evidence in the region for the killing of adult mammoths in quantity with great stones.[11] This then is one reason for the aggregation of people at the site. But it is simplistic to expect that mere need for cooperation in hunting was the reason—indeed the principal reason—for the concentration of pop-ulation assumed for Dolni Vestonice. It is quite probable, in view of the chances of preservation, that the settlement was somewhat larger than that which has been revealed so far. The site of Pred-mosti, which was probably settled contemporaneously with Dolni Vestonice, covers some 2½ acres. Since it was badly excavated, the nature of the settlement is unknown, but it probably had twice the population of Dolni Vestonice.

Man is a social creature, and it is society that creates the special environment which allows men to interact in a meaningful way. An examination of other Gravettian or Gravettian-like sites elsewhere shows other economic emphases than mammoth hunt-ing, proving that whatever the animal selected, reindeer, bison, horse, or mammoth, and whatever the cooperation required in that selection, the social capability for that cooperation was already ex-istent. It is this fact that haunts theories of economic determinism from Karl Marx to V. G. Childe. The excavator Klima states this Marxian view in just so many words:

All the members of the primal community formed a single indivisible economic unit, a common production organiza-tion. Only this type of formation would have been capable of assembling a group sufficiently numerous and strong, given the then available means of production, to secure the enormous hunting yield attested by the vast bone accumulation. The formation is also attested by the very fact that a mighty pachyderm like the mammoth could be conquered at all and that its dissected parts could be transported to the settlement. This explanation, derived from an interpretation of the upper portions of the station at Dolni Vestonice, essentially agrees with the generally accepted image of the life in the permanent settlements of the upper paleolithic.[12]

What is critical is the fact that the thousands of years which mark the span of the Paleolithic also mark the evolution of human society. The simple familial band of Terra Amata had had 300,000 years of both physical environmental and social challenge to select out the factors for social change which by Gravettian times had produced new forms. Just as stone tools had changed because of man's increasing awareness of new potentials in tool usage, so man had arrived at other ways of organizing society. Two inimitable pressures had always challenged social life: the need for cooperation among growing populations of individuals and the incest taboos, however they were applied to human relations. The evidence that the Gravettians were *Homo sapiens sapiens,* mentally as capable of dealing with abstract conceptions as modern man, makes all the more important the awareness that the men of Dolni Vestonice were at least equally concerned with the social condition of man as with his economic or technological status.

As compared to the human communities discernible on the rim of human terrestrial time, such as that of Terra Amata, the people of Dolni Vestonice were more numerous and their society was more than just familial, even in the band context. Certain assumptions can be made, then, about social organization.

It is clear that the hearths at least were the center of attraction in each hut. If they were used for cooking as well as for warmth, for which there is some evidence (burnt bone), then it is possible

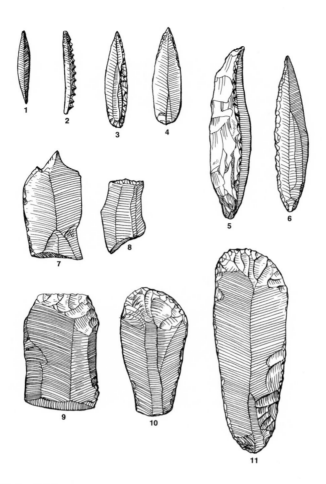

Upper Paleolithic stone tools of Europe. 1: point; 2: sickle or saw blade; 3–6: knives; 7: awl; 8: burin; 9–11: scrapers.

to assume that the cooking fires were used on a familial basis. The family, then, would have to consist of more than just its nuclear members of father, mother, and their children, both because of the large size of the hut and the assumed population of the settlement as a whole. Among the band systems of social organization known to ethnologists, the vast majority are of patrilocal type; that is, the male brings his wife to the father's place of residence. A good reason for this is that cooperation in hunting and defense is a male requisite, especially since the males are often far afield and need one another's help in a dozen situations. Thus the family tends to cluster its males, whereas women can be married into another family, thereby binding that family through kinship without losing the male aggregation. In such situations women replace one another in each family through marriage. The family, then, is at once exogamous and virilocal. From this kind of evidence, one can assume that each hut contained the families of brothers and their relatives in the male line. Thus if each hut was the residence of a patrilocal group it is probable that there were marriage ties to the other families of the settlement. The individual eligible male then had female relatives with whom he was resident but whom he could not marry: his sister and his parallel cousins (his father's brothers' daughters). His wife-to-be must be chosen from females outside the hut who were unrelated or from his cross cousins (mother's brothers' daughters), who of course were not normally resident in his hut. In a settlement the size of Dolni Vestonice, such distinctions gave every individual a social identity which bonded him to others in the settlement on a kin basis. Since the death rate was high (only one in ten reached the age of forty, and a third of the population died before twenty) the few males and females surviving beyond the age of thirty may well have obtained special distinction and their kin bonds particular prestige. It is of interest to note that in each hut there are larger and smaller hearths suggestive of different sizes of family unit in each—perhaps a response to the high death rate.[13]

The whole settlement, then, can be presumed to be made up of eight to twelve families (assuming two brothers each with a family of about four as the average), patrilocally and probably patrilineally distinct but through exogamic practices bound together on a recognized kinship basis.

Leadership

The wall which is presumed to have enclosed the whole living area of the settlement emphasizes its social unity. However, in addition to kinship and the need for cooperation in economic activities, there have to be other socializing factors to make the group continually cohesive. One of these is leadership. Cooperation in the hunting of large game needs a pole about which it can revolve. Evidence for individual leaders is nonexistent at Dolni Vestonice, but the grave of an adult male uncovered at the Gravettian site at Brünn implies a degree of leadership permanence. The individual was buried wearing a necklace made up of six hundred dentalium shells, and on his person were numerous discs of mammoth bone and ivory. With him in the grave was an ivory male figurine which was legless and had but one arm. The skeleton was stained with ocher and the whole grave covered with rhinoceros bone and mammoth tusks. The man was obviously a person of distinction, and one might hazard the suggestion that he was a leader in some activity which gave him special prominence.

Band society, as pointed out in chapter 4, is naturally democratic in its choice of leaders. The talents of the individual are always tested and the leaders that emerge are those whose successes make their leadership obvious. One type of leader is the one who coordinates the activities of the men in such situations as defense or hunting. Another leader role is that of keeping the young instructed in the values and skills of the group. Here the surviving elders, as well as the individual fathers and mothers, have their roles. Under no condition can the individual operate against the cohesiveness of the group, so that in the fullest sense all who lead lead for group purposes. Prestige is gained for the individual only when that individual succeeds in a task which the group recognizes is of collective benefit. Leadership in band society functions on a temporary basis, and prestige gained through leadership is always tested against new tasks. Personal ambition in such circumstances never exceeds the limits of group ambition. At Brünn, however, leadership appears to have been given permanence in recognition of the individual's success.

Dolni Vestonice is thus apparently representative of a different type of society from that of Terra Amata, in that it had a greater degree of permanence in leadership, it was larger in population and more complex in character, and its social cohesiveness was dependent on more than mere familial membership. It is thus possible that the seasonal shifts took place in one of two principal ways. The people of the settlement may have moved as a unit to the plains, perhaps following established routes at the end of winter, or they may have broken up into family units at the hut level and so dispersed into traditional hunting-gathering territories until winter's impending onset brought them back together again. Both types of migratory movement are known to ethnologists.

Relations with Other Settlements

It is clear that Southern Moravia was well populated with Gravettian settlements. In addition to Dolni Vestonice there are the known settlements of Pavlov, Brünn, and Predmosti, and there is evidence for others. The evidence establishes no fundamental differences between the settlement of Dolni Vestonice and the other Gravettian settlements. Since none of these sites is more than fifty or so miles from another, contact between them or their inhabitants at various times was probably common. Perhaps these contacts could have been aggressive as hunting and gathering grounds were quarreled over, but this seems unlikely in the context of what is known of primitive man's relationships generally. What probably brought the ancient settlements together were the kin relationships that made possible organic cooperation among them. Thus each settlement was united in a web of kin ties which allowed the individual a group membership and which may have related him to other groups. He must have given a name to that group—his band, his settlement.

The study of the primitive mind which has been one of the major pursuits of anthropologists has brought forth the fact that primitive man makes no clear distinction between the natural and the supernatural. To primitive man they are essentially equal in

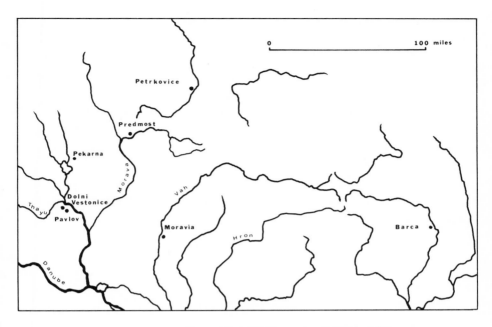

Gravettian Settlements of Central Europe

their being necessary to the state of being. This is never so clear as in the sense that death is merely a movement of the spirit from immediate perception to another level of perception. The family is then not only of immediate concern to the living but of concern to all those who have died and to those that will come. Nor is the family concerned only with the men and women past or present that have made it up, for the individual's very awareness of things beside the perception of people makes him include manifestations of nature as well. "Is not that old tree which my forefathers knew a part of my family?" Out of this consciousness of the interdependence of things, not only in time but in space, springs one's special relationship to a particular animal, plant, rock, or even the wind and the sun. It is a real relationship, as vital as one's blood kin to one's security and identity. Such a relationship is known as totemism, and it is often graphically symbolized in figures of wood, stone, or other material. But it is by no means a simple matter of image or symbol acknowledgment. The totem is a part of one's cosmology, and it has a place in the order of things. This place can be acknowledged through individual or group rites. The acknowledgment is the means by which all things are assured of order in the universe.

The totem is often familial and is given a kin name, such as uncle, father, or mother. Each family may have its totem and the whole band a totem of its own. The totem is characteristically thought to have an ancestral or generic role, which is recounted in myth and elaborated in legend. Totemism is another cohesive factor in the life of the group. It is characteristic of primitive life and thus can be assumed to have been a factor at Dolni Vestonice. Perhaps there were totemic relationships to the mammoth, the principal food animal of the winter camp. In any case the settlements which were in contact probably had different totemic ancestors, which they acknowledged ritually. Totemic relationship is of course as valid as blood relationship; thus it would be incestuous for individuals of the same totem to marry. It appears that if the patrilocal group had a common totemic ancestor for all its members it had to practice exogamy, and thus intergroup relationships might have included intermarriage. This of course has regional meaning.

The problem is that there is no clear evidence for these relationships. How much was the cohesiveness of the larger group necessary in summer? On the face of the evidence it is probable that dispersal of the family units in summer and congregation of the units into settlements in winter was the order of life. Yet if there were a number of large settlements, territorial agreements and migratory routes might have had to be worked out for mutual subsistence benefit and the reduction of intergroup aggression. Groups are, however, most effective when they are small in size, since they can scavenge in a given territory and survive even when times are difficult. Larger groups have to be constantly successful in their hunting and gathering, for there are more mouths to feed. On the open plains the mammoth herds were difficult to approach. There were few cliffs from which to drop stones, and pit traps would hardly be effective where dispersal was the order. Yet small mammals and abundant plant life provided plenty of food for the family and the need to aggregate was minimized. So long as men were not belligerent to the point of mutual aggression they were able to function as a familial economic group.

Hypothetically, then, the families reunite in the traditional winter camps, still keeping a degree of separatism but united because they are related by marriage and perhaps by totemic ancestor, because they have a need to cooperate in hunting the nearby congregated big game, and because they are willing to share leadership at a critical time. This sharing also extends to tools, to know-how in making things, to reciprocity in the procurement of pelts, food, and raw material, and to wall, hut, and fire building. One can call this type of social organization a *compound band,* or even an elementary tribe, in that it consists of a number of large families which seasonally cluster for purposes of cooperative function. While they acknowledge kinship and share leadership rites, beliefs, and technology, each family unit is essentially discrete. The winter camp also involved another major cohesive element— religious belief and ritual identification.

Religion and Ritual

Western civilized man has as one of the bases of his scientific vision the taxonomic ordering of both reality and all else that he might comprehend. Everything fits somewhere in an orderly and largely evolutionary scheme of things. Nature of course does not have a consciousness of Western man's ordering of the cosmos, and for that reason taxonomic divisions are constantly changing when behavioral characteristics do not equate with the structural characteristics by which they were first categorized.

Primitive man tends to order the phenomena of the world on the basis of behavior, often using analogy as a means of describing the phenomenon at hand. If a thing is "like a rock," what is meant is not merely that it has rocklike hardness or color or shape but that it shares an innate and identical quality with the rock. This attitude can extend to human emotion, indeed to human activity of all kinds.

Man is one with nature; he is within nature and is moved by it. In this conception historical consciousness has no part, for what one can conceive as having occurred long ago in a golden age of gods happens in the present because he who lives in the present conceives the happening now in spite of its apparent temporal remoteness. Myth which accounts for the nature of the world is told and retold, acted and reenacted, and its symbols are regarded as simply an abstraction of reality.

The world of primitive man can be compared to a sphere with the individual somewhere in its midst. Inside this sphere the parameters are always drawn wherever one happens to be at any moment of the daily or seasonal temporal cycle. They constantly change, and one's consciousness of position is always dependent on a holistic view that includes the physical perceptions and the nonphysical awarenesses: the combination of that which the senses reveal and that which the mind perceives. It is ultimately as religious to make a stone ax, trap a lizard, bear a child, or fall asleep as it is to wear an amulet, talk with spirits, recite a myth, or perform a ritual. It is part of the same cognition.

This knowledge of the primitive world view makes possible a reasonable approximation of the cosmological consciousness of prehistoric man and of the men of Dolni Vestonice in particular. The presence of animal and human figurines and of a variety of other artifactual materials of Gravettian type—a type generally familar in Central and Eastern Europe—provides a starting point. For it is clear from the distribution of these forms that there were themes which were held in common among the Gravettian people. Indeed it is increasingly apparent that the Central European Gravettian represents an *oikoumenē* (a unified cultural region) and that it had a diffusionary role in influencing much of Upper Paleolithic Europe.

There has been for some time a grave uncertainty as to the meaning of Paleolithic art. For a long time it has been assumed by prehistorians that the art bore upon religious beliefs in which magic, invocation, ritual hunt, dance, sacrifice, and totemism had roles. There have also been a number of historians who saw in the art the beginnings of that aesthetic expression apparently a necessary part of the makeup of *Homo sapiens* which eventually was to lead to the great art expressions of historical time. The French prehistorian André Leroi-Gourhan has classified Paleolithic art according to stages of its development: primitive, archaic, classical; this classification provides an understandable framework by which to measure its development much as one would any historical artistic school. In the case of Paleolithic art, however, the time span is not less than 20,000 years. Leroi-Gourhan sees the primary motivation for the art as sexual, and he divides it generally into male or female, based on his study of the symbolism involved.[14]

More recently Alexander Marshack, an American anthropologist who has found plausible evidence for systems of lunar and other notation from at least 25,000 years ago up to the beginning of food production in Western Asia, has argued that the art should be interpreted as representative of the early development of abstract thinking—in effect, of that process of cognition which is the basis of civilization.[15]

Many prehistorians have agreed that there is a degree of abstraction both in the figurative and the cryptic signs found in both the parietal and the mobile art of the Paleolithic. But abstraction is not limited to art. The abstraction process which relates meaning to graphic representation is identical to that which assigns meaning to the sounds which emanate from the human throat—in effect, with the development of language—and to that which recognizes color. Cognition goes beyond understanding by analogy; it involves meaning for meaning's sake, and this can only be brought about coherently through the use of mutually intelligible symbolization.

An examination of the rich repertoire of stone, bone, and pre-

served wood tools and weapons of the Gravettian and an awareness of the processes they represent, the consideration of the complexities of social, economic, and even political life where status
and value are involved, would warrant the conclusion that considerable vocabulary must have been used to cause men to operate ef-
ficiently and cohesively within the culture. It would have to include names for animals, plants, and materials, place names,

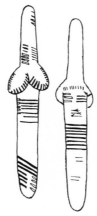

Markings on a bone
found at Dolni Vestonice.

personal names, familial names, and possibly totemic names. Abstract words for marriage, death, birth, menstruation, age, brav-
ery, and cowardice are probably of ancient vintage. The very cultural complexity designated artifactually, or intrinsic in the size
and character of the settlement, indicates a measure of abstract oral
symbolism. Cognition through abstraction, no matter how limited,
was thus inherent in daily and seasonal life. Ideological belief was
as much a result of the complexity of daily and seasonal life as it
was a reflection of the cosmology acknowledged at the time.
Those who argue that an increasing knowledge of symbolism as it
was used for ideological purposes or for purposes of notation demonstrates an evolutionary step towards civilization are basing their
views on but one aspect of what has to be regarded as a total development to which all elements of the culture contributed. This is
never so clear as it is in the religious area. The holistic conception
of man in nature marks the mind of primitive man.

Art, Women, and Prehistoric Ideology

The Gravettian heyday was earlier than the great periods of Western European cave art; in fact there is virtually no cave art east of the Alps. It is in the little sculptures of animals and especially of human females—the famous Venuses—that Gravettian "art" is manifest. The question then is why did these people make this "art"? The answer is that they did so because that "art" had a role, one might venture to say an important role, in the workings of Gravettian culture. It was graphic representation of belief in the interrelatedness of all things—a belief noted by anthropologists in the study of many cultures:

Eskimo: "Essentially the relation of society to nature was mediated by a series of symbolic representations and actions increasing an individual's feeling of security in a hostile environment." [16]

Pygmy: "At no time do their songs ask for this or that to be done, for the hunt to be made better or for someone's illness to be cured; it is not necessary. All that is needful is to awaken the forest, and everything will come right." [17]

Australian Bushman: "Economics, art, and religion are mutually interdependent, and to understand the hunting and food-gathering activities demands also an understanding of these other aspects of life." [18]

Andamanese: "The explanation of each single custom is provided by showing what is its relation to the other customs of the Andamanese and to their general system of ideas and sentiments." [19]

Samoyed: "I suddenly felt like a child and, as in childhood, I imagined that every object had its spirit, that water and air were populated by mysterious invisible beings who, in inexplicable fashion, ruled the course of the world and the fate of men." [20]

The Venus figurines share in common general facelessness and limblessness, amplified breasts, large buttocks, and pregnancy. Wherever they are found they are associated with habitation debris; in the case of Dolni Vestonice the figure was found in the large exterior hearth in the midst of the settlement. It is clear, then, that whatever the function of the figurines they were a part of everyday activity and were not isolated from it, as appears to have been the case with much of cave art which is found in the depths of caves far from the places of habitation. This suggests that the figurines were as secular as they were sacred. Some of the possibilities which the association indicates are set forth in Table 3 (Appendix).

In view of the holistic character of primitive man's cosmic vision, it is difficult to assign the Venuses to religion alone. Whatever their function, it is worth repeating that they had a cohesive role in the culture. Furthermore, one can reasonably assume that the Venus as a symbol was linked to the *idea* of pregnancy as well as to the physical presence of it. Thus the abstract as well as the material were involved. This is perfectly consistent with the complexity of mind which modern ethnology has confirmed for primitive man.

In a larger sense there is a mysterious quality about women's ability to bear children to which such modern phrases as "the eternal woman" bear contemporary witness. *Homo sapiens* was probably rarely naive enough not to know that the sexual act was necessary for procreation. Yet that of itself explains nothing. The child that emerges from its mother's womb is a complete entity—a duplication in kind of adult and child alike—the product of a mysterious force at work within the womb. The sense of the miraculous adheres to the birth of a child even in our time. It can be assumed that the same sense was present even more intensely in the heyday of Dolni Vestonice. While such an assumption cannot be proved, it can be accepted by ethnological analogy.

Mammiform beads on necklaces found at Dolni Vestonice and other sites of Gravettian vintage provide further evidence of female centrism of some kind. A famous tusk representation of a female has long been known since it was found at Predmosti just east of Brünn. It resembles in its execution the bark paintings of the

Stylized "Venus" carved
on a tusk, from Predmosti.

Australian aborigines—a hint perhaps of a much-used material not preserved in the remains of the Paleolithic.

Specialists in the Supernatural

The special burial of the facially deformed female and the two representations of her indicate another aspect of ancient belief. In many societies of the world the deformed, the afflicted, and the aged are regarded with considerable awe. They are accredited with supernatural powers either of their own doing or as the earthly representative of the unearthly. Such individuals play a variety of roles in a society, from soothsayer to sorcerer, from saint to witch. Among primitive societies there is always someone who represents the supernatural in some way. Because the primitive mind does not make a clear distinction between sacred and secular, natural and unnatural, it often happens that the societies' religious practitioners are temporary—the individuals reverting back to normal when the supernatural manifestation is ended. All the individuals of the society, then, are thus potentially exponents of the supernatural—and in fact all claim and participate in religious experience of intense and often dramatic kind. In societies which are undergoing constant stress because of physical environmental factors or are in states of change or unrest, it often means that certain individuals, because of physical or mental (assumed or unassumed) handicaps, are unable to take up their share of the daily work load. These individuals—who otherwise might be shunned, often with fatal consequences—take their place in society by advertently or inadvertently undertaking the responsibilities of dealing with the supernatural. Since the supernatural is a very real concern of daily life, the individual who has communication with—or power over —the supernatural has an important role to play in the secular world. Some practitioners heal ritually, others prophesy, and still others practice magic, including sleight of hand as well as making amulets which protect, energize, or amplify the abilities of the individual. One person can indeed have all these roles in one.

There is evidence that the sprinkling of red ocher on the flesh or bones of the deceased is a ritual act intended somehow either to restore the red blood of life to the deceased spirit wherever it may be or in some way to relate the living and the dead ceremonially.[21] This custom is evidenced in Neanderthal burials in the periods prior to the Gravettian settlement of Central Europe and is common to burials of Gravettian population there. It is clear both from the presence of red ocher and the funerary accompaniments in many of those burials, as well as their deliberate nature (indicated by such features as special covers, contracted position, and proximity to the living), that men of the Upper Paleolithic of Europe had a belief in some form of afterlife. Most probably this involved the belief that the spirits of the dead hovered near their bodies for good or evil—or perhaps that they traveled afar taking with them the emblems they had worn or won among the living so that they would resume their utility in another world.

The woman of Dolni Vestonice with her crooked face and special burial suggests that she was regarded with certain ritual awe in life, which continued after death. Was she given to strange actions in keeping with her abnormal look? Actions which proclaimed her supernatural contacts and abilities? One cannot know, of course, but at the same time one can be reasonably sure that in the eyes of the inhabitants of ancient Dolni Vestonice she was no ordinary woman. Her distortion was copied in ivory and her body carefully interred *within* the settlement—a situation given to no other in the same context. The presence of the bones of the arctic fox in the grave attests to a certain relationship between the deformed body and that animal. Was it her special patron—her contact with the supernatural? Was it the special totem of the settlement—the people of the fox? Was it a sacrificial animal meant to placate or accompany the dead? Again there is no answer. The presence of a missile point in the grave suggests sacrifice. Thus we have the tantalizing evidence of associational attributes of ancient burial: deformed woman placed in her grave in a certain way, sprinkled with red ocher, accompanied by a fox, and having as weapon a spearhead. Furthermore she is remembered in graphic imagery. It takes no imagination to understand that the people of Dolni Vestonice were under constant stress owing to cold, danger, disease, food needs, and a sense of powerlessness in a world where the supernatural was all-powerful. That they were well adapted to survive in the physical world is clear from the material evidence of the settlement. It may not be too speculative to consider the woman of Dolni Vestonice as evidence for successful adaptation to the supernatural world, analogous to other examples attested to by ethnologists. (It is noteworthy that Marshack found traces of red ocher in marks on a female statuette from Dolni Vestonice. Life and female may thus have been related symbolically.) [22]

The semisubterranean hut outside but close to the settlement and quite clearly part of it is evidence for a special activity which the hearth-oven it contains helps identify. The absence of habitation debris but the presence of over two thousand figurines and figure fragments, as well as ambiguous lumps, which were baked in the hearth-oven, clearly emphasizes that these figurines were important to the life of the settlement. It is unlikely in view of the times that the figurines were mere toys. Most of them are depictions of the animals or parts of animals known to the Pollauan people. They are very good depictions. As with most prehistoric art, the concern is with the essence of the animal—size, strength, bold shape, prominent features—rather than realistic illustration. In this sense the figurines are abstracts, yet the intention is obviously to depict what the hunter responds to in the animal. It is likely that the figurines served some special purposes, such as amulets. (The Netsilik Eskimo wear as many as seventy amulets at a time as protection, for luck, and for strength.) There is some indication that such figurines were deliberately stabbed, as if to kill sympathetically the prey one sought and thus to insure the actual kill contagiously. Such explanations are the rather stock answers of prehistorians to the problem, and they are given some validity by ethnographic analogy.

Whereas many Paleolithic figurines are made in bone and ivory and probably more were made in nonpreserved wood, these are made in baked clay. The clay was easily obtained from the surroundings. It is clear that whoever made the figurines was familiar with the properties of clay and the need for tempering, for limestone particles were mixed into the clay before it was modeled and baked. Furthermore, the hardness of the baked clay is evidence for some control of the air supply fed into the hearth-oven. Some of the "flutes" found in the hut may have been blow tubes used in concentrating the air supply in the hearth-oven—probably involving several individuals. Perhaps this hut of more than 25,000 years before the industrial revolution is an ancestor to the great steel mills of today, where the concentration of air and fire in a closed space for the purposes of hardening or softening material is identical in purpose.

Cultural Evolution

The presence of a ceramic industry at Dolni Vestonice (including the Venus figurines) is indicative of an acceleration of a developmental process in the Upper Paleolithic generally. Whereas some three hundred thousand years separate the culture of Dolni Vestonice from that of Terra Amata, it is less than twenty thousand years from Dolni Vestonice to the early civilizations of Sumeria and Egypt and only a few thousand years more to our time. Something was operating in the human experience to accelerate certain processes, cultural or otherwise. It is in this perspective that the cultural character of this period is of special interest, particularly in its Central European context.

The French prehistorian François Bordes sees typological relationships across Europe from France to the Ukraine and thus asserts the possibility that the French Perigordian (an Upper Paleolithic cultural assemblage) was ancestral to the Central European and Ukrainian "Gravettian." [23] The Venus figurines and many of the stone tool types are reasonable evidence for this. One important fact emerges from the studies of the Upper Paleolithic of Europe, and that is that though there were numerous industrial traditions in the period after at least 40,000 years ago there was a great deal of continuity, overlap, and simple contact. It has been pointed out that the cave art of France and Spain is basically one great tradition changing stylistically through time, in which such famous Upper Paleolithic traditions as the Aurignacian, Perigordian-Gravettian, Solutrean, and Magdalenian, all had a part. [24] The wonderful grave remains of Grimaldi on the Italian Riviera, which include elaborate funerary furniture, ocher staining, double burials, and the like, are thus as much a part of the European Upper Paleolithic tradition as are the fine paintings of Lascaux and

Altamira and the oval shelters of the Ukraine, some of which measure a hundred feet in length and may represent a communal life of considerable magnitude. The end of the Mousterian industries, which are associated generally with Neanderthal man, came about in Europe generally around 35,000 years ago. For the next 25,000 years the traditions of the Upper Paleolithic were dominant. This dominance took place in a climatic situation like that described for Dolni Vestonice with the warmer, more temperate areas naturally near the sea and south of the Alps. In those 25,000 years the innovations of one region were diffused to another, producing eventually Europe's first great *oikoumenē,* an *oikoumenē* which had as its outstanding features:

- elaborate and sophisticated hunting-gathering tools and techniques.
- sizable communities of one hundred or more.
- social organization which depended increasingly on leadership by individuals more permanently elevated than hitherto. These leaders were involved in religious as well as economic activities.
- longer life expectancy. (Neanderthal man had a life expectancy of only twenty years.)
- special emphasis on certain animals for food according to region.
- much plant food for which certain tools and processes were developed.
- a rich graphic expression.
- belief in some form of afterlife for which ritual preparation was necessary.
- seasonal movements of considerable scale but within traditional territories. Seasonal movement in many areas probably emphasized dispersal in summer and concentration in winter.
- specializations not directly related to subsistence obtainment, such as sewing, modeling, baking clay, sculpturing, painting.

- notational ability.
- symbolism recognizable from region to region.
- emphasis upon human females as representative of some critical aspect of human continuity.
- social organization which was most likely patrilocal with emphasis upon the extended family and extra family relations.
- open-air settlements with the large tent-hut as the characteristic shelter—each with hearth or several hearths. Cave and rock-shelter settlements, however, were common.
- many settlements located near rivers or other bodies of water, thus the setting for intercommunity relationships.

Central Europe in the heyday of Gravettian occupation was fairly heavily settled. If Dolni Vestonice is a good sample, an estimate of from 1,000 to 3,000 people in the area from Predmosti south and west into the Danube Valley seems reasonable, and this is perhaps an underestimate. Some degree of interaction between the groups of people who made up this population is implicit in the general uniformity of industrial and settlement habit which has been unearthed so far. In addition to social interaction it is also fairly clear that the rivers of the region were the foci of winter settlement and the plains and hills the areas of summer emphasis. (Unfortunately, no summer campsites have been found for this region. Traps and fishing gear are not so far evidenced, but either or both of these techniques are reasonable to assume.) The ecological differences between these areas of seasonal interest required different hunting and gathering techniques, and thus diversity of seasonal subsistence-seeking methods may have been motivational in the acceptance of change generally. Thus the reasonably rapid innovations of the Upper Paleolithic in this and other regions may have taken place in an atmosphere of changing ways. Suffice it to note that the settlement of Dolni Vestonice is not representative of a static level in the story of man but one which presaged the elaborations which brought about truly settled life.

Cognition Stage

One cannot help but be struck by the evidence for process at Dolni Vestonice and adjacent sites. The blade tool industry is not simply the consequence of purposeful flaking of nodules of stone but is the result of a thoughtful planning in response to technological needs. There is a cognitive sequence leading from a spectrum of technological needs—to plan—to applied skill—to product—to product use. Thus such processes as flaking primarily and secondarily, hafting on a material already chosen and carved for the receipt of the flaked object, resulting in a compound tool which required skill to use, were normal parts of Gravettian industry. The baking of clay, the construction of walls, the relationship of individuals to recognized superfamilial functions, notational abilities, and the creation of forms by which to represent qualities of existence have to be placed alongside the purposeful selecting out of the young of mammoth for a staple in the diet as well as a presumed similar selectivity in regard to edible plants. In the latter case the sickle blades and the grindstones familiar at Dolni Vestonice are graphic evidence for a complex process of plant exploitation and possible plant food preparation in which the process of grinding, mixing, and cooking (baking, boiling) are involved. Similarly, the relationship of individuals such as the deformed woman to mythic narratives used to explain natural phenomena escapes us, but her presence underlines the strong possibility that some such explanative system was present.

Social organization and social relations generally were not simple. There was the nuclear family, the extended family (the band?), and possibly the compound band and the tribe. To all these social units the individual had some obligation. Furthermore, each compound band or tribe was in the proximity of another such group, in the winter months at the least. The scale of the world about was large in winter and vast in summer, for within a hundred miles was encompassed the varied terrains of plain, hill, great and small river valley, high mountains, forests, marshlands, and passes which have made Central Europe so important in history. This, together with an equally varied biota, had the effect of extending a material world consciousness far beyond one's settlement or traditional seasonal routes. An equivalence in concepts of the supernatural is in keeping with modern knowledge of the existential conceptions of primitive man. One striking piece of evidence in this context is found in the widely distributed but similar Venus figurines.

The men of Dolni Vestonice were enactive still in meeting the material challenges of the environment. It was largely a matter of immediacy, in which the individual was required by strength of arm or leg to obtain food or fight danger. His weapon and tool kit emphasized sharpness rather than heft, and in this there was advantage. The spear or the lance was a marvelous innovation but he did not possess the bow—a still more advantageous tool for hunters and one which would have its role in causing future change. In toolmaking, however, the planning factor had as its motivation the image of a completed tool of some complexity and dependent on a logical series of more than one discrete step. This image-planning-action relationship was also to be found in cooperative action under a leader, in the celebration of rites whose aim was to influence the supernatural, in the maintenance of individual and collective identity amid the complexity of social relations, and in the perception of one's place in a far-flung teeming world whose bounds no one individual might physically expect to reach but which collectively all were made aware of by the larger society of men which in one's life cycle came out of unknown terrain into the familiar.

Thus it is clear that the characteristics of an ikonic culture were manifest in many of the categories of the Gravettian. The milieu of the individual was largely the physical world, in which hard work, risk, duress, and an early death were the lot of most. Yet there was a larger than familial social environment to which the individual had special obligations of respect, cooperation, conformity, and affection. In fulfillment of these obligations the individual received knowledge, support, sustenance, security, and entertainment. In that context conceptions of other states of action and being than one's own were made possible. It is obvious, then, that Dolni Vestonice represents a giant step on the path to civilization.

6

Prelude
to a New Life

SOME TWELVE THOUSAND YEARS AGO the Pleistocene drew to a close as the glaciers retreated into regions where their traces are still found today. It had been a gradual process of brief advances and longer retreats begun millennia before, but the end result was that by about 7000 B.C., in much of Europe at least, a forested landscape appeared with the tundra confined to the north. The climate was now temperate. The animal life of tundra days had largely disappeared, first such large game as the mammoth and bison herds, then the reindeer, leaving the wild cattle, boar, and deer known to Europeans almost to modern times. Europe is a continent of great geographical diversity, and as a consequence habitats vary widely. In this period of slow environmental change tundra, steppe, woodland, and parkland locales might exist side by side and within each a characteristic biota, including man and his particular cultural adaptations.

Western Asia is also a land of considerable landscape diversity. If one moves from the Mediterranean coast of Palestine northeastward, one encounters in order (1) a low, narrow, somewhat rainy coast; (2) a moderately high coastal range of mountains; (3) upland valleys and plains; (4) a great depression in which there are a series of saline rivers, lakes, and seas; (5) a vast upland desert plateau; (6) a riverine flat valley; (7) foothills with some rainfall; (8) upland valleys and plains; and (9) high mountains—beyond which are vast desert and semidesert regions. In the Pleistocene there were montaine glaciations in the foothills, which fluctuated in patterns similar to those of Europe but with local variations. Towards the end of the Pleistocene the climate of most of Western Asia appears to have approached that of today: wet and cool uplands and dry, warm lowlands with a great variety of differing subclimates between and with these concurrently a great variety of ecological microzones. The whole region, but particularly the uplands, was the seat of a broad spectrum of plants and animals which included forms which were in time to be domesticates of man. From the Balkans to Afghanistan and Turkmenistan across the Anatolian Plateau and the ranges of the Anteles and the Zagros could be found, in wild form and in differing quantity, goats, sheep, cattle, pigs, horses, barleys, wheats, and other usable but apparently never domesticated species such as the gazelle, deer, snail, and turtle. Legumes, acorns, pistachio nuts, and lentils were also native. Some of the stands of wild wheat as well as the wild herds of cattle were thick, and in the former case it has been stated that a family could harvest in three weeks more than enough to feed itself for a year.[1]

A significant difference existed between Europe and Western Asia as well as Northern Africa at the end of the Pleistocene. In the latter two cases the temperate and watered zones were next to relatively narrow areas, marginal to truly arid regions, such as the Arabian and Saharan deserts and the Iranian plateau. In times of greater or lesser rainfall the marginal areas expanded and contracted. The marginal areas were thereby always in a state of flux, while the essential desert and upland environments remained the same. Europe, situated largely in a temperate zone, by contrast has no great arid region within its bounds, though areas such as the interiors of Spain and mainland Greece are subject to near desert conditions. Europe is divided by the Pyrenees, Alps, and Carpathians into two great halves: a northern which drains essentially to the Atlantic Ocean and the Baltic Sea and a southern which faces on the Mediterranean and Black seas. The northern is a flattish open and forested land while the southern is replete with subranges, hills, rocky coasts, and great inland valleys, the vast plain of the Hungarian puszta being the exception. In all, Europe has a more varied geography than does Western Asia. One consequence of this in human terms is the fact that Europe as early as the Middle Paleolithic had considerably more diversity in certain cultural features than did Western Asia. This continued well into historic times. As was pointed out in chapter 5, the Gravettian of Europe had many regional aspects, and these were symptomatic of the diversity caused at least in part by local adaptation to the many different regions of Europe from France to the Ukraine. In comparison, Upper Paleolithic industries are relatively few in Western Asia and tend to be quite homogeneous. Farther east, in India and China, there is even less diversity in comparable industries, many of which appear to have evolved directly from older indigenous ones.

The Mesolithic

The term *Mesolithic* refers to those industries and cultural assemblages identified as having been present in Europe at the close of the Pleistocene and in the several millennia following. They are generally considered to represent post-Pleistocene adaptations. The European Mesolithic contains the essential diversity that one would expect. The cultures of the Mesolithic are those of hunters, fishers, and gatherers beautifully adapted to their environment—which could be the shore of an ice-melt lake, the seacoast, the edge of a forest, the edge of a marshland, or the bank of a river. Their life was generally one of movement from place to place on a seasonal basis in the time-honored way. Their commu-

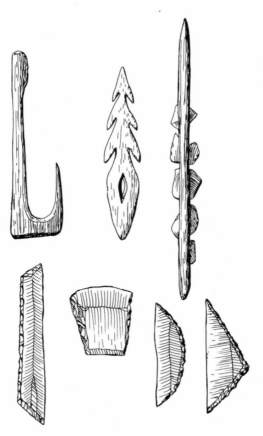

Mesolithic tool kit of Europe. *Top:* wooden hook, bone harpoon, and a club made of hafted blades. *Bottom:* small knives and scrapers made on stone blades.

nities were smallish (less than a hundred) though as in the Upper Paleolithic a given region might at any one time support a considerable number of their settlements.

In a comparable time period Western Asia presents a general uniformity of hunting-gathering cultural assemblages which vary but little. Two of these assemblages, the Natufian of Palestine and the Karim Shahirian of northeastern Iraq, contain grinding stones, polished stone celts, and sickle blades. There is evidence that these people ate wild or semiwild goats, sheep, and cattle, as well as using wild grasses (including the cereals) in their diets—a not surprising piece of evidence in view of the fact that representatives of this fauna and flora were abundant in the region of settlement.

In reviewing the archaeological evidence for the period, it becomes clear that man wherever he is found was in control of his subsistence resources in the sense that he was thoroughly aware of seasonal change and animal habit and was a master of the techniques by which to obtain the maximum results within the capability both of his empirical knowledge and his evolved technology. Some have called this control-awareness an intensification of hunting-gathering and speak of it as a kind of reaction to the challenges of the post-Pleistocene landscape. From this intensification was to spring the origin of domestication. Some have argued that domestication took place because population pressure moved groups out of the optimum hunting-gathering areas into marginal zones where, in order to survive, man had to exploit the indigenous plants and animals intensely.[2] This is similar to Toynbee's challenge and response hypothesis. Provocative as this idea is, it seems to assume that optimum conditions are necessarily inimical to innovation. On the contrary, the stress factor can prevent the experimentation which the optimum area permits.

Evidence for the Great Transition

Shortly after World War II, R. J. Braidwood of the Oriental Institute of the University of Chicago began the direction of a series of field investigations in the Near East which were to have enormous importance to the study of the origins of civilization. Braidwood's objective was to obtain archaeological evidence for the great transition from a life of food gathering, which had marked the inhabitants of the prehistoric world, to that of food production, which created and supported the village life of the Near East and out of which civilization emerged. "From cave to village" was a slogan often used in describing Braidwood's goals. The region chosen for field examination was Iraq, the site of the world's earliest known civilization, that of Sumeria. Previous investigations of the region had shown that not only were there cave and open-air sites of the Paleolithic—what Braidwood calls the food-gathering stage—but numerous village sites representative of many later periods as well. Deep excavations of certain sites lo-

DANUBE

MEDITERRANEAN

Europe and Western Asia

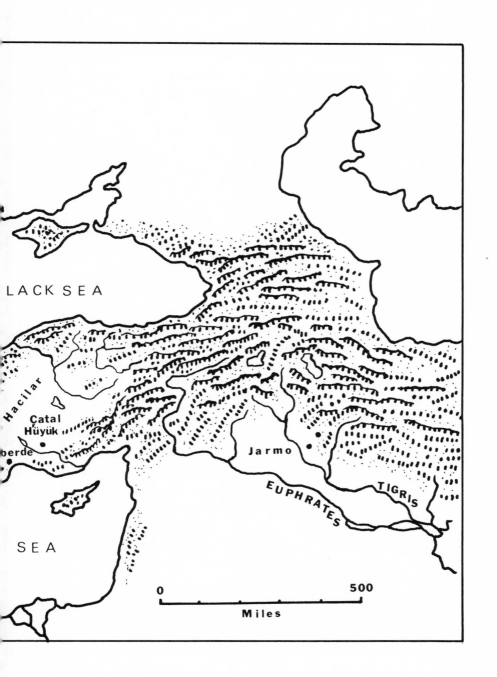

LACK SEA

Hacilar

Çatal
Hüyük

berde

Jarmo

EUPHRATES

TIGRIS

SEA

0   500
Miles

cated in the lower Mesopotamian plain indicated that occupation there was quite late. In contrast the foothills and higher plains—which lie parallel to the high mountain ranges east and north of the fertile plains of the Tigris-Euphrates drainage—yielded numerous early sites, including some village settlements containing ostensibly primitive assemblages of artifacts. This transitional region of higher rainfall and limited but fertile soil Braidwood refers to as the "hilly flanks" of the Fertile Crescent, the alluvial lands which run in a vast crescent from the marshes of the Tigris-Euphrates delta to the Nile Valley, and which include the Levant.

Important in the selection of the hilly flanks as the zone of concentration was the fact that there was evidence that the zone was what Braidwood described as a natural "nuclear" area. This means that in the hilly flanks could be found indigenously wild forms of sheep, goats, pigs, cattle, and perhaps horses as well as the cereal plants wheat and barley—in other words, most of the species which when domesticated became the subsistence foundation for settled life in the Near East. Most of these are present there in wild form today and the presence of the others is known archaeologically.

Braidwood brought into the field not only archaeologists like himself but natural scientists whose researches on the problems of identifying the beginnings and early forms of domestication were vital to the solution of the main problem. Most notable among these scientists were the American mammalogist Charles Reed, the paleobotanist Hans Helbaek, and the geologist Herbert Wright. Multidisciplinary scientific expeditions have been known for many years. One has only to think of Napoleon's expedition to Egypt, the various government expeditions sent by Europeans and Americans to the Antarctic and other regions of the world, and the famous Roy Chapman Andrews expeditions to Mongolia. Archaeological expeditions had tended to be single-disciplinary, however, and consequently much evidence had been overlooked.

Braidwood's team produced abundant evidence for stages in a transitional scheme "from cave to village." An important site in the Braidwoodian scheme was that of Jarmo—a site some 4 acres in extent, located on the edge of a bluff in the Kurdish hills east of Kirkuk. This site produced evidence for early (transitional) forms of domesticated wheat and barley and for goats, sheep, and pigs. Jarmo's houses were permanent but small and limited to a population of about seven per house. Some twenty houses were occupied at a time to a total estimated population of 140–150, hardly larger than that of Dolni Vestonice. As at Dolni Vestonice there were figurines of animals and of humans—even of a pregnant "Venus." The stone tools were numerous but diminutive in size—many made of obsidian, which could only be obtained from a place some 300 miles away. Radiocarbon dating, which was only recently developed when Braidwood dug at Jarmo, averaged out to 6750 B.C. ±200 years.

The importance of Jarmo was and is its reflection of a way of life seemingly transitional between hunting-gathering and full-fledged dependence on domestication. Relative permanence of yearly settlement is one of the obvious and important differences between the life styles of Dolni Vestonice and Jarmo. The people of Jarmo were hunters and gatherers but they were also agriculturalists, no matter how primitive. At Dolni Vestonice the habits of the mammoth were motivational in setting the length of time and the season of the year in which the settlement could be occupied. At Jarmo agriculture was the prime motivator—thus the longer duration of settlement; it may well be, however, that a certain amount of movement still occurred owing to a subsistence pattern responsive to the rhythms of the season, the requirement for raw materials, and the need to escape the rigors of local climate.

In Jarmo and at other sites discovered by Braidwood and his colleagues was the evidence for at least part of probably the most momentous change in human history. From sites such as Jarmo one can trace the often faint but still discernible trail that leads sequentially to the dawn of civilization.

Braidwood refused to use the older terminologies such as *Mesolithic* and *Neolithic* to describe the stages of development as

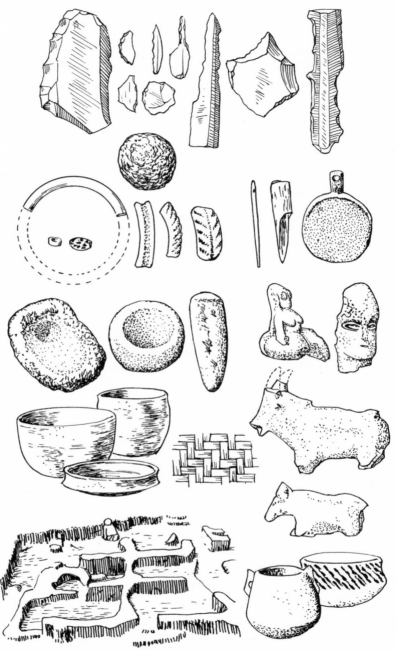

Findings at Jarmo. *Top row:* flint knives, sickle blades, and scrapers. *Second row:* stone ball; bangles of clay, bone, and shell; small beads; bone needle and point; pendant. *Third row:* grinding stone, mortar and pestle, clay human figurines. *Fourth row:* pottery vessels, basket weave, animal figurines. *Fifth row:* earthen wall plan; pottery.

he and his colleagues saw them. He preferred a terminology which would express more concisely the relation of man to his subsistence-seeking emphases. Thus for the Middle Paleolithic of the Near East he used the term *generalized food gathering;* for the Upper Paleolithic *food collecting,* meaning a more intensified usage of a given environmental zone; between the *terminal phase of food collecting* and the *primary phase of food production* (domestication) he used the term *incipience* (era of incipient cultivation); finally the dawn of settled life came under the term *primary village farming*—the last, of course, being well represented by Jarmo and comparable sites. For each of his stages Braidwood presented archaeological sites in the hilly flanks as candidates.

Braidwood's scheme has naturally been modified, expanded, and embellished in recent years, but as of this writing it still represents the most coherent scheme of its kind.

Braidwood's initial work took place just before Sputnik alarmed the American people to such an extent that millions and millions of tax dollars were poured into the National Science Foundation and its counterparts "to catch up." This had a major influence on the expansion of universities throughout the country; the seemingly unlimited government funds stimulated the growth of departments of anthropology and the consequent appearance of a plethora of excellent graduate students with an interest in the kind of problems Braidwood sought to solve. Numerous NSF-backed field expeditions rushed to Iraq, Syria, Iran, Egypt, Anatolia, and adjacent regions. Braidwood's multidisciplinary approach provided motivation for activity in all the sciences—hard and otherwise.

The result of all this activity has been the production of a mass of new archaeological evidence and related nonartifactual material. New theories have been set forth, some based on statistical handling of both kinds of data, and the Braidwood scheme has been both severely criticized and highly eulogized. What emerges, however, are two outstanding facts, both of which were anticipated by Braidwood. The first is that there were other nuclear areas both in the New and Old Worlds than that of the Near East and that within at least some of them the manipulation of potentially domesticable plants and animals was carried on in a time period not too remote from that of the Near East—in some cases successfully, as rice, maize, the water buffalo, the llama, and the reindeer may bear out. The second is that this period of intensive relationship with potential domesticates, Braidwood's era of incipience, was of considerable duration, more than the two or three thousand years (10,000–7000 B.C.) originally set forth.

A third fact, not apparently anticipated, was that though sites like Jarmo might represent a primary village phase in the Kurdish hills, not all villages of that phase were as small or indeed as primitive as Jarmo. One of the first disputes with the Braidwood scheme came from the English archaeologist Kathleen Kenyon, who in digging the mound of Tell-es-Sultan at Jericho in Palestine found a large settlement surrounded by a stone wall over 12 feet high, complete with a tower which must have risen over 30 feet, and enclosing an area possibly some 10 acres in extent. The terms *town* and even *prehistoric city* have been assigned to this level at Jericho. The point is that a date comparable to that of Jarmo was assignable to Jericho; furthermore, Jericho was not up on the "hilly flanks" but down below sea level in the valley of the Jordan near a perennial spring—in a kind of oasis. Another site comparable in size to Jericho was discovered up on the Anatolian plateau by the English archaeologist James Mellaart—Çatal Hüyük, which will be the subject of the following two chapters. Other smaller sites than these two, comparable to Jarmo in size and of the same level of development, have been found from the Balkans to Central Asia, and there is a good chance of comparable small sites in Egypt.

The important work of the American anthropologists Frank Hole, Kent Flannery, and James Neely in the Khuzistan of Iran (Deh Luran plain) produced evidence of a sequence from Braidwood's terminal food-gathering to primary-village and later phases and set forth a model of what may well have been characteristic of the great transformation in the Near East generally. Apparently, at the end of the Pleistocene (c.10,000–9000 B.C.) the basically steppe land environment of the region was divided up naturally into at least five microenvironments. Since the region receives winter rains of some volume, there are marshes, streams, rivers, and a considerable growth of vegetation in both the surrounding hills and the alluvial plains (which of course varies seasonally). The abundance of vegetation was attractive to grazers and their predators, and thus in the era of food collecting hunters and gatherers exploited the various microenvironments in which they found the game and the plant food they sought.

Around 7000 B.C. cultivators arrived, bringing with them emmer wheat, two-row hulled barley, sheep, and goats—all of which appear to have originated in higher regions. The fact that these species had been so domesticated by now as to permit their movement into another environment than their native one is indicative of the success cultivators of the time were having in their domestication experiments, pragmatic as they probably were.

Apparently the initial cultivation practice was limited to the winter months, when there was rain and good grazing on the steppe plain. In the summer season the settlers moved their herds to upland meadows. This habit eventually became unnecessary, owing to the fertility of the Deh Luran plain. Thus sedentarization set in and the slow development of permanent settled life there began.[3]

The sequence in Deh Luran does not evidence Braidwood's era of incipience nor does it document the great concentration of population at the primary-village phase demonstrated at Jericho and Çatal Hüyük. It does, however, comment on the closeness with which men and environment interacted, resulting in the achievement of sedentary life. At the earliest phase of sedentarization some twenty-odd forms of plant life, both wild and cultivated, were identified; at least thirteen species of wild and domesticated animal life are known for the same period.

In Palestine a cultural assemblage called the Natufian has been known since the 1930s, when it was first identified as the uppermost habitation level in the series of caves at Mount Carmel. Since

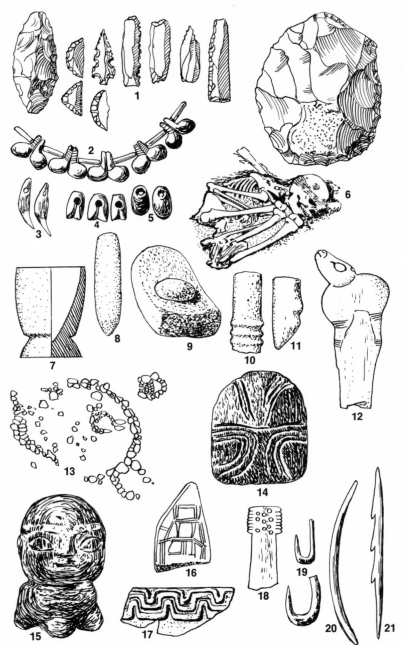

Natufian findings. 1: blade tools; 2: mammiform beads on necklace; 3: beads of animal teeth; 4, 5: beads; 6: flexed burial with shell head-dress; 7–11: ground stone objects; 12: bone animal figurine; 13: Natufian structure with stone foundation; 14: stylized figurine; 15: stone sculpture; 16, 17: design motifs; 18: bone or ivory wand (?); 19: hooks; 20: needle; 21: harpoon point.

then it has been found to be widespread in the region. The Natufian people appear to have flourished around 8000 B.C. and lived not only in caves and rock shelters but in small huts in the open air as well. Some of these had storage pits. They even occur in the lowest levels of Tell-es-Sultan at Jericho beneath Miss Kenyon's walled "town." The Natufians hunted gazelle and deer, with an emphasis on the former. From what is known of the habitats of these beasts it can be said that the climate of 8000 B.C. was much like today's in Palestine—dry and somewhat hot—but with considerable microenvironmental variance.

The Natufians buried their dead near their residences, often with necklaces and shell headdresses—apparently to adorn them for the other world. They had a bone industry turning the raw material into a variety of fine needles, fishhooks, and harpoon heads. They carved animal and human figurines, and some of the mammiform beads on the necklaces are similar to those of Dolni Vestonice. They ground stone and used mortars and pestles. In the midst of a rather elaborate stone tool industry made up largely of tiny blades of various forms were found sickle blades. On the latter was a sheen which is caused by the friction set up by hard contact with the stems of wild cereal plants and other grasses. This evidence and the possibility that they had a domesticated dog of sorts has caused Braidwood to assign the Natufian to his era of incipience. The sickle blades at least would seem to evidence the fact that these ancient people realized the nutritive value of some of the wild cereals and were among those ancients who were manipulating the forebears of domesticated cereal—the food basis of settled life. A similar assemblage to that of the Natufians has been found in northeastern Iraq and is known as the Karim Shahirian, proving that this experimentation was widespread.

The Causes of Domestication

But what caused domestication to occur? Incipience requires man and the potential domesticates to be in proximity as a first premise, but the second by definition is that domestication must precipitate out of the first. As pointed out in chapter 5, there is evidence that as early as 25,000 years ago men were selecting out certain animals and plants as the basis of their subsistence. The whole Upper Paleolithic of Europe and Western Asia is generally demonstrative of this tendency, and the Mesolithic or terminal food-gathering era which follows is equally demonstrative of it. But selection does not mean narrowing down to the extent that other forms of subsistence were ignored. It does mean that men tried to remain in proximity to their subsistence ideal—that is, to whatever was the main staple of their diet. On this basis empiricism would make it possible to replace a main staple with something comparable should the need arise. There are numerous sites in the stratigraphy of the Upper Paleolithic that demonstrate this fact: men did not move away from their "natural habitat" but made every effort apparently to replace staples with others. True seasonal migratory routes changed and territories shifted as the game supply waxed and waned, but archaeological evidence testifies to man's effort to stabilize his life within a known environment. Thus as early as Terra Amata there is evidence for a basic stability—a return year after year to a given camp on a seasonal route. When men have a broad spectrum of subsistence support they have alternatives should a dietary favorite fail. It would appear that this broad spectrum emphasis has been a basic principle for over a quarter of a million years. Its motivation is based both on assuring a food supply and on balancing the diet, the former purpose empirical, the latter perhaps innate in man as an omnivorous primate.

The fashion of selecting out a given plant or animal as a staple of the diet is probably on the one side due to the abundance of that form and on the other due to the ability to obtain that form for food: for the mammoth, it depended on cooperative hunting techniques geared to mammoth behavior; for wild cereals, it depended on the sickle, the grinding stone, the vessel, and the fire. It is highly unlikely that there were fewer elephants in Europe in the

Middle Pleistocene or that wild cereals were not found in flourishing stands hundreds of thousands of years ago. The ability to exploit these resources fully, however, was lacking. The slow evolution of technology had to be accompanied by a similar evolution of cultural behaviors conducive to innovation and the recognition of consequence in all areas of cultural life.

Thus it can be said that the Natufians or Karim Shahirians were no different from the people of Dolni Vestonice in their selecting certain animals and plants out of the spectrum of dietary possibilities regularly available to them. In fact, as indicated in chapter 5, sickles, grinding stones, fire—and very probably wooden vessels—were known to the people of Dolni Vestonice. The mammoth hunters were committed to seasonal movement based on the cycle "mammoth meat in winter—plant and other animal food in summer." The people of Natufian type, however, not only could reap wild cereal plants in a short intensive period of the year but were able to *store* the abundance obtained. A degree of permanence was possible in this habit.

All this does not explain the reasons why domestication appears *when* it did. It does explain why it appears *where* it did. The nuclear-area concept explains one part of the answer; the other part relates to the character of cultural evolution and the growth of cognition. Man must have reached a stage in his awareness of his universe which opened new perspectives. If indeed stability in all parts of human existence is the natural goal of the individual and his society, then there has been motivation in cultural evolution which explains utopian yearnings and the thrust towards "omega." It also explains the emergence of settled life based on domestication. In this sense the appearance of farming and the village ethos can be said to be the fulfillment of the ultimate quest of the men of the Stone Age—no matter how subconsciously. All that had evolved before in the growth of understanding made possible the great transformation: The increasing complexity of social life, leadership roles, moral order in human relationships, abstract concepts of fertility and other phenomena, the objectification of aspects of the cosmos, notational abilities, and the improvement of technological skills were all necessary parts of that evolution. Collectively they culminate in a cultural potential. This potential, placed within a biota containing that which was potentially domesticable, began the "great transformation." The transformation not only depended on the domestication of that which was domesticable but also required the emergence of new cultural values, different social forms, special leadership, innovative technology, and a world view in which settled life was given its raison d'être.

The Role of Genius

The act of innovation and change as the consequence of "genius" is amply illustrated in the history of science and literature, "genius" being used here to refer either to specific individuals—the Einsteins and Edisons of prehistory—or to a creative capacity shared by a number of people whose idea exchange led to fundamental innovations. A major controversy in anthropology has been the role of the great man in history—does he move his times or is he a product of them? In the present context it should be obvious that both cultural readiness and individual capability are involved.[4]

It appears that as the result of the deliberate and conscious actions such as a craftsman or farmer performs in observing and working materials, certain often illogical elements of his experience are lodged in his subconscious, where they remain hidden and stable for unknown periods of time. In cases where the conscious search for answers is continued, some of the hidden elements fall into patterns which emerge often as sudden inspirations or visions. These inspirations give rise to further conscious and deliberate effort to produce a concrete result. The degree of inspiration and the production of an eventual innovation or material response is dependent on the "genius" of the individual involved; however, the initial gathering of data is definitely related to the conscious search for it—and often to the interaction of individuals in whatever environment: physical, social, or intellectual. Large interacting populations, for example, motivate the exchange of ideas and produce the potential of innovation on every side. Innovation does not occur, however, until "genius" produces a workable model which in turn must be accepted or rejected by the society involved. Settled life based on animal and plant domestication required, then, deliberate and conscious manipulation of the known elements of the physical, social, and intellectual environments which permitted empirically derived and observed data to be stored in the subconscious of men of "genius"; some of this data one day configured and emerged as the basis of innovation. What degree of "genius" was involved is of course unknown. But the level of cognition is definitely related to the question, for not only does the innovation potential have to be recognized, but a conscious understanding of consequence is involved. Here the society's need for change is critical. Something has to operate to make people conscious of new values to their life; otherwise innovation, no matter how viable to the outsider, is rejected or ignored. In the case of domestication the evidence from the Gravettian example would indicate that there was great cultural potential for the development of settled life based upon some aspect of domestication. In turn it can be postulated that men of "genius" had due inspiration but that in the context of Gravettian cultural cognition the innovations leading to settled life of the kind later found in the Near East were rejected. This is to say then that as men explore, manipulate, and understand their universes of physical, social, and intellectual properties innovative ideas are continually bred as the natural productivity of the advanced capability of the brain of *Homo sapiens.* The fact that these ideas appear to have rarely gained root in prehistoric times is a consequence of the lack of sufficient cognitive development of society at any one time. With the larger interacting populations and more complex cultures in such Upper Paleolithic context as the Gravettian *oikoumenē,* there was not only a higher level of cognition but an intensification of conscious manipulation of all aspects of culture. Out of the manipulation by means of the conscious-subconscious-conscious evolution of idea within the brain of men of "genius" came the innovative models some of which, accepted by society, made critical change possible and thus permitted new cognitive environments to emerge as the breeding ground for ever newer models, which in turn would be accepted or rejected according to cultural readiness.

Although the nuclear area was in Western Asia, the evidence is that the cultural potential for its exploitation came from Europe. The achievements of the Upper Paleolithic in the varied environment of that continent were far in advance of anything so far known in the same period in Western Asia. (In this sense the European Upper Paleolithic experience parallels that of Western Asia's great transformation. As Marshack puts it: "Might the question of why various agricultures evolved 'suddenly' in a limited period of a few thousand years out of apparent Upper Palaeolithic roots be related to the question of why art and symbol developed 'suddenly' in the Upper Palaeolithic? Were both aspects of a developing cognitive and cultural complexity? We are brought again to the problem of the contents, meaning, and nature of human knowledge." [5])

One of the hallmarks of the European Mesolithic is that tool kit of diminutive blade tools collectively called microlithic which apparently appears first in Western Europe and then diffuses eastward. This kit emphasizes the compound tool, one of the major innovations of ancient technology already presaged in the Gravettian technology. (Even if it should be established that microliths appeared earlier outside Europe, their widespread appearance in a comparable time period illustrates more than casual contact.) It is not the kit itself, important as it is, that needs emphasis here, but the fact that its rapid diffusion in the critical period (11,000–8000 B.C.) underlines the reality of diffusionary channels between Europe and Asia. It is thus no coincidence that there are stylistic parallels in the Natufian assemblage of artifacts to that of Dolni Vestonice.

There seems little question that the arid lowlands and plateaus of Western Asia tended to keep men in the highlands, where natural resources were far more abundant. Not that there were no cultures adapted to the deserts, oases, and marginal arid lands—archaeological evidence proves otherwise. However, the evidence also shows that a greater number of subsistence seekers were to be found in the hilly flank zones. The hilly flanks were not only well inhabited but, via Anatolia and the Balkans, were the bridge lands to Europe. Thus as a nuclear zone, as a center of population, and as a bridge land, the highlands of Western Asia qualified as the setting for the next stage in man's movement towards civilization.

The site of Çatal Hüyük in Anatolia illustrates a culmination of primary village life in which are compounded the achievements of the older hunting-gathering way of life with the new developments.

7

The Site
of Çatal Hüyük

The Setting

THE EXTRAORDINARY SITE of Çatal Hüyük is found in the center of
the fertile Konya-Eregli plain near Cumra in south central Anatolia. The location is about 3,000 feet above sea level in a region of
interior drainage—a physical characteristic of much of the central
portions of the lands of the Near and Middle East. In this case the
river Carsamba flows out of the Beysehir, a lake of the Taurus
Mountains (which are on the west of the great plain), bends to the
south, and then comes abruptly north again to disappear in arid
steppe lands. Çatal Hüyük is located at that strategic riverine point
where the Carsamba, meandering over the increasingly flat plain,
breaks into the branches of its blind delta. Çatal Hüyük lies alongside the middle branch (now dried up).

The site is actually a double mound straddling the old river
course. The western mound is the smaller and later of the two and
has been investigated only cursorily, but the eastern has been
called "the largest neolithic site hitherto known in the Near
East." [1] It covers some 32 acres and rises over 50 feet higher than
the modern plain surface. Soundings indicate that it may actually
reach a yard or two below the plain, owing to accumulation of

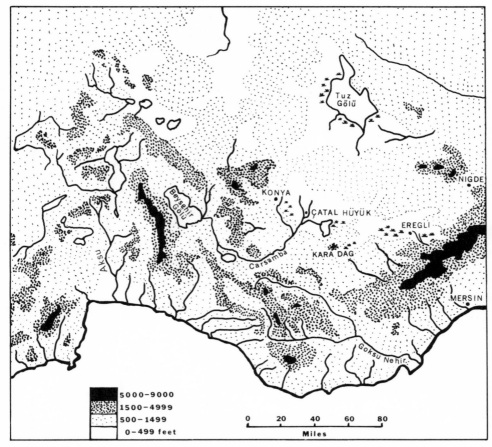

Konya Region, Anatolia

soils on the surrounding area.[2] Situated as it is in the midst of the most fertile wheat-growing region of modern (and indeed ancient) Turkey, the survival of Çatal Hüyük is in itself worthy of comment; but most remarkable is the fact that what survives of the eastern mound appears to be almost entirely of Early Neolithic vintage; that is, it represents a period that *ended* around the middle of the sixth millennium B.C.

The Excavations

It has been fortunate that the discoverer and excavator over four seasons (1961–63; 1965), the British archaeologist James

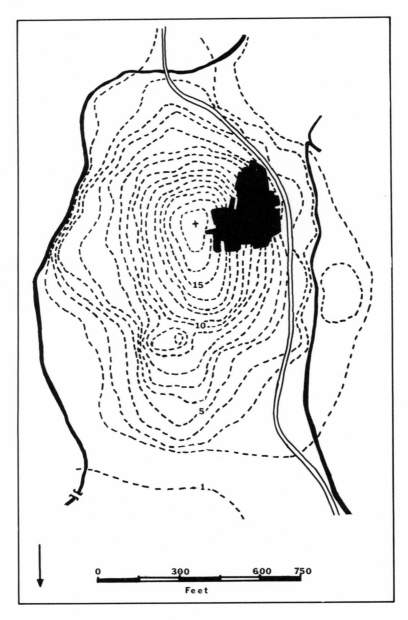

Site of Çatal Hüyük

Mellaart, has so sensibly and sensitively carried out one of the most challenging archaeological tasks of recent years. Mellaart has brought into the field teams of natural scientists and conservators as well as excavators whose individual and collective efforts have produced and preserved the largest array of documented material of this period so far obtained—material that includes painted murals, wooden vessels, and carbonized textiles, as well as plant and animal remains. It is because of this excellence of field technique that Çatal Hüyük provides such a reliable model.

Mellaart was able to excavate a little over an acre, or about a thirtieth of the whole. He has determined twelve distinct levels of occupation without yet reaching the bottom of the cultural deposits. (The work has been stopped since 1965.) Of these levels the sixth and fifth are best known because they were the most extensively excavated; however, the excavator finds comparatively little cultural change from lowest to highest discernible levels (or earliest to latest). Radiocarbon dating indicates that the site was occupied between 6500+ B.C. and 5600 B.C., after which Çatal Hüyük West was inhabited for almost another thousand years.

The Architecture

The excavator's general comment on the buildings uncovered sets the impression for the whole:

> Orderliness and planning prevail everywhere; in the size of bricks, the standard plan of houses and shrines, the heights of panels, doorways, hearths and ovens and to a great extent in the size of rooms.[3]

The unusual conditions of preservation enable the reconstruction of the houses on a scale unique in prehistoric archaeology. The evidence indicates that the inhabitants constructed rectangular, flat-roof houses in which were rooms as large as 500 square feet but more commonly averaging 20 by 15 feet. The builders ap-

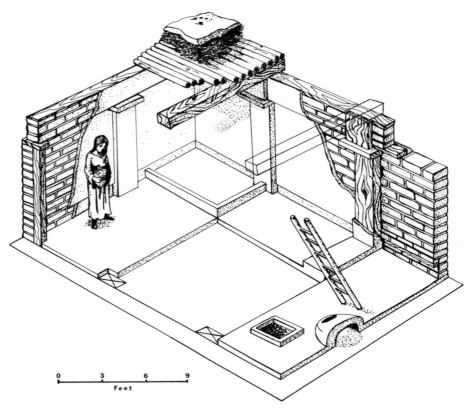

0   3   6   9
Feet

Typical Çatal Hüyük house (reconstruction).

parently used hands and feet as the standard of measurement. Houses in the Near East, both ancient and modern, are typically made almost entirely of mudbrick. The houses of Çatal Hüyük are framed in timber (oak) arranged in post-and-beam fashion and free-standing. Mudbrick was used to fill the openings between the posts. To lessen the distance of the roof opening the walls were stepped inward. Beams were laid across, then layers of red mats, and finally mud. A white plaster was used inside to coat the walls and platforms. The walls were frequently painted with "murals," often multicolored. Small subsidiary rooms—apparently for storage—could be reached only through the main room of each house. These rooms contained bins for grain or storage boxes for a variety of objects of daily usage.

The interior of the house had its own conventions, the most obvious of which were the raised platforms that ran around three sides of the main room. These platforms, except on the south, were apparently for sleeping and general living activity. The southern platform was the kitchen area; here were found the hearth, the oven, and the fuel storage alcove. Here also was the place of the ladder to the roof, the only exit—the hole in the roof thus serving as smoke hole and entranceway. It is suggested that a kiosk or cover of some kind was placed over that hole to prevent its being too blatantly open, which for a number of obvious reasons is disadvantageous.

The settlement, then, was made up of these flat-roofed houses which were side by side, sharing walls and occasional courtyards, where by the way were the waste disposal sites. The inside of the houses were, according to the excavator, kept "scrupulously clean."

Significantly, though there were small windows for light set high on the walls in clerestory fashion, the physical aspect of the settlement was one of general blankness. It is speculated that the collective individualism of the settlement, offering no opportunity to an invader except the difficulty of moving from house to house in whose dark interior awaited an armed defender, would be as formidable a reason not to attack as any formal outer wall might be. In any case one gets the impression from the clustering quality of the houses that there was a decided and emphatic motivation to stay together. Of interest in this regard is the attitude of the Hopi Indians of the Southwest of the United States whose mesa-top village homes are very similar in character to those of Çatal Hüyük. Here the reasons for the clustering are very clear: labor and space. Space because the village is confined to a mesa-top, and labor because walls are shared when houses are contiguous.[4] It does appear that the latter reason at least is applicable here. The physical cost of preparing the wooden posts for the houses, which in most of the occupations were squared (as were the ladders), may very well have motivated wall sharing.

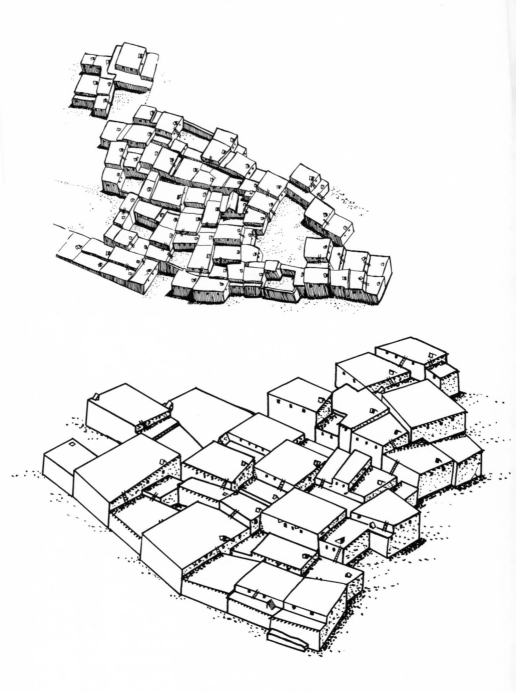

Çatal Hüyük (reconstruction): *top,* Level VI-B; *bottom,* Level VI.

In order to provide more light, however, the houses were turned about and even terraced on the slope of the mound. A second story made up of perhaps lighter building materials may have existed for some houses, and there are occasional exceptions to the flat-roof habit in gabled chambers, perhaps a reflection of a tradition of building reed structures as well as those of wood and brick.

The Objects of Daily Life

The objects found are summarized in Tables 4 and 5 (Appendix)—over seventy categories of what are in most cases obviously the pragmatic artifacts of daily life, a daily life which included the hunting of game, perhaps the herding of domesticated animals, the gathering of usable plants, and most certainly the cultivation of cereal grains. The appearance of objects made of copper and lead, small as they are, is of great interest, for they are expressive both of a recognition of the qualities of metal and the beginning of experiments to produce them from the ores in which they are hidden. Halet Çambel and R. J. Braidwood found evidence for cold-hammering and grinding of native copper at the site of Cayonu Tepesi in southeastern Iran in a chronological context just prior to 7000 B.C.[5] The site is located in a region rich in copper ores, and the material was therefore right under the inhabitants' noses, so to speak—a fact of considerable importance in the development of ideas as to utility.

The presence of evidence for weaving is of some interest, not only for the fact that the people were capable of doing so but because weaving involves counting. It can be said that there is a direct correlation between complexity of weaving and sophistication of arithmetic understanding. This is further emphasized by the precision by which buildings were laid out and constructed. Bricks, for example, which were mold-made and sun-baked, were, if modern parallels are at all valid, never manufactured in numbers beyond needs. In other words, men knew precisely how many bricks were necessary for each wall. There are numerous other examples of this type which can be assumed from the evi-

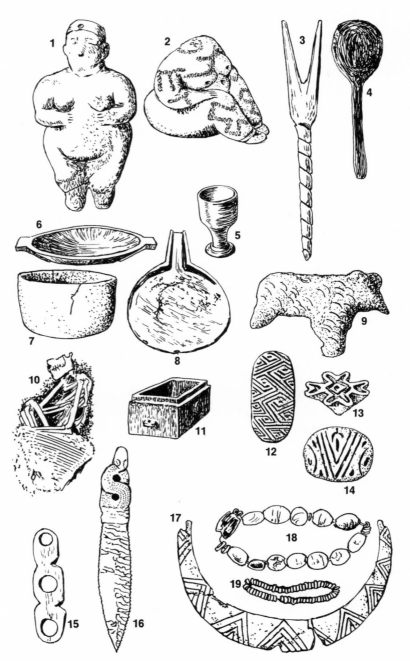

Çatal Hüyük artifacts. 1, 2: clay human female figurines; 3: forked tool; 4: wooden spoon; 5–8: objects in wood; 9: clay animal figurine; 10: flexed burial; 11: wooden box; 12–14: stamp seals; 15: wooden object of unknown use; 16: snake handle knife; 17: decorated collar; 18, 19: necklaces.

Statues and figurines at Çatal Hüyük. 1: painted clay female figurine; 2: "goddess" between two leopards, giving birth to a human child; 3: paired male (?) and female carvings; 4: female sculpture in the round; 5: stylized human figurine.

dence, including the very great possibility of a calendric system of notation available to prehistoric man.[6] It all adds up to the fact that counting and notation were very much a part of the cultural scene at Çatal Hüyük.

Sculpture and Painting: Clues to Religion

The most dramatic feature of the discoveries at Çatal Hüyük is undeniably the abundance of decoration and ornamentation caused

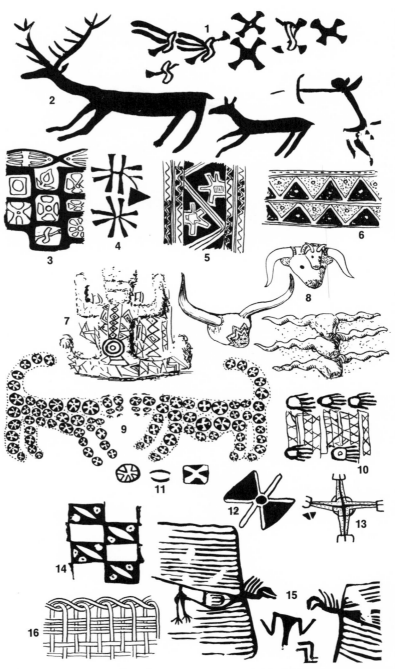

Typical motifs used in Çatal Hüyük paintings and modelings. 1–6, 9–15: motifs used in wall paintings; 7, 8: wall modelings of animals; 16: diagram of weaving technique.

by the presence of clay and plaster reliefs—some over animal skulls—and colorful wall paintings, which characteristically occur on all walls but that of the utilitarian south. Benches and pillars embellished with cattle horn cores neatly plastered form handsome and rather awesome features of certain rooms, while commonly in the panels formed by posts are painted geometric, floral, and other stylized symbol patterns suggestive of woven wall hangings like the kilim rugs of modern Turkey. Striking bands are formed by human hands pigmented in black or red, appearing either as part of a composition or standing alone. The reliefs are largely concerned with bovines, rams, and an occasional leopard, stag, or "goddess"—or parts thereof; the paintings not only include these but add macabre scenes of great vultures attacking headless or hapless humans and jovial scenes of hunting and dancing in which men in leopard-skin caps dash about or wave their arms and leopard-skin-clad individuals flourish bows and maces while deer hurriedly attempt to leave or great bulls stand motionless. Frequently a dog appears; lions, boars, a crane (or stork) or two, animal and human corpses, a drummer, a dance, and even a scene of an erupting volcano add to the corpus of what at the present time has to be considered the most important group of prehistoric paintings after the earlier ones of Western Europe. Mellaart sees convention in the placement of the decoration:

> It appears that the decoration of shrines followed certain rules; scenes dealing with death are always placed on the east and north walls, below which the dead were buried. Scenes dealing with birth occupy the opposite west wall and bulls are found only on the north wall facing the Taurus Mountains, perhaps not a coincidence. Animal heads associated with red painted niches are always on the east wall but goddesses and bull and ram heads have no special place and may occur on any wall.[7]

A wide choice of colors was available to the painters of Çatal Hüyük, from black and gray to blue and green, with red and

The vultures and the dead, a typical Çatal Hüyük wall painting.

The dancers, a scene from the Çatal Hüyük hunting shrine, level III.

brown being favored. Paint was applied by brush, rag, and crayon techniques.

It appears to have been traditional to plaster over a house interior at intervals, including the paintings and reliefs, which were sometimes replaced and sometimes not. As many as a hundred layers of plaster or whitewash have been found in some cases. It is suggested by the excavator that this replastering occurred on an annual basis, thus providing a standard by which to measure the age of a house.[8] When a house was too old its roof and upper walls were pulled down, and the debris set within the stubs of the old walls formed a foundation for a new structure. If the older building contained extensive decoration, the new building would also.

Mellaart and his colleagues separate the rooms of excavated Çatal Hüyük into two main categories: ordinary dwelling rooms and shrines or cult rooms.

> Out of 139 living rooms excavated at Çatal Hüyük II–X, not less than forty and probably more, appear to have served Neolithic religion. Such cult rooms or shrines are more elaborately decorated than houses and they are frequently, but not always, the largest building in the quarter. In plan and construction they are no different from ordinary dwellings and they include all the familiar built-in furniture, such as platforms, benches, hearths and ovens which we have already recognized as an integral part of the Çatal Hüyük building-tradition. Burials are also common in shrines, but there are some notable exceptions; none were found in the shrine of Level II or in the second shrine of Level III.[9]

Mellaart established eight principal criteria for identifying a shrine:
- Presence of elaborate wall paintings of an "obvious ritual or religious significance."
- Plaster reliefs of animals, animal heads, or deities.
- Horns of cattle arranged as parts of benches.

- Bucrania in rows.
- Groups of "cult statues" in the main room.
- Votive figures placed in the walls.
- Human skulls on platforms.
- The presence of ocher-stained burials, which apparently were placed only in shrines.[10]

According to these criteria Mellaart sees the settlement—or at least that part so far excavated—as consisting of greater shrines (those which are larger and more richly decorated), lesser shrines, and ordinary houses.

The "cult statues" were made of a variety of materials of varying hardness from clay to marble and including stalagmitic limestone derived from caves in the nearby mountains. The clay figurines are largely of animals. These were deliberately stabbed and cached in pits as if to ritually invoke good luck in the hunt through sympathetic magic—a ritual belief already old by the seventh millennium B.C. (see chapter 5).

The stone cut figures or statues are largely of women with some emphasis in the sculpturing on breasts, stomach, and hips but not on the genitalia. Features are often merely suggested by the shape of the natural stone fragment, occasionally reinforced by a strategic incision for mouth or eyes here and there or modeled by grinding. Some of the figurines cut in the same style were found together in a "shrine." One such group consists of three statues: two of women and one of a boy. They all ride leopards. Occasionally a group of two or four figures were modeled out of or on a single stone. These show mother and child or perhaps a sexual embrace. One such sculpture has two forms of a "goddess" with but a single pair of arms between them.

One of the most provocative of the statues is made of baked clay. It is of a substantial female seated between two cats, probably leopards, while from her womb emerges the head of a human being. This little figure was found in the grain bin of a "shrine," suggestive of a relationship to the produce of agriculture if not agriculture itself (herself?).

Leopards appear to have been a popular and meaningful theme among the statue makers, for they appear in a variety of ways—as riding animals, as aids to birth, as dresses, and even as cubs dandled by the large-hipped and large-breasted woman conventionally modeled. There are also representations of plant designs on the dresses of these females; such evidence coupled with in situ location in the "shrines" suggest again a relationship to agriculture. Then again the woman appears with the vulture which, if the murals of preying vultures are any indication, were regarded as birds of death. Mellaart has observed the appearance of modeled human breasts on the walls of "shrines" which, far from promising life-giving milk, contain the awesome jaws and tusks of such predators as boar, weasel, fox, and vulture. Incorporated into amuletic form, females of this type also appear in graves. The excavator thus has evidence for the role of a female of supernatural quality in all aspects of the cycle of human and animal life.

Males in comparison seem to have a minor role in the beliefs of the time. They appear in statuette form as sons of the "goddesses," as husbands (associated with bulls), and as hunters (associated with the leopard).

The Cult of the Dead

Burial customs give a vivid clue as to ideas of a spirit world. When an individual died, his body was exposed until the elements and the vultures had cleaned away the flesh. The skeleton was then wrapped in cloth or animal skin and buried under the platform within the house, where it usually joined previous burials, for the solitary grave was the exception rather than the rule. Apparently one was literally buried in death where one had slept in life: adult males on the northeast, women and children (usually) along the main platform on the east wall. Normally the convention of burial in a contracted position on the left side was observed. Most burials were plain and giftless except for containers of food. Where gifts do occur, the women are served better than the men, for they have cosmetic kits, much jewelry in the form of necklaces, rings, pins, bracelets, and pendants, and beautifully ground obsidian mirrors. Then, too, there are tools of daily life, such as the hoe, the knife, and the sewing needle.

Men, on the other hand, have little jewelry but plenty of weapons and objects necessary for the hunt as well as sickle blades for reaping grain, and hooks, eyes, and toggles for fastening clothing.

The burials with obsidian mirrors, as well as those with bone belt fasteners (for leopard-skin robes), are also confined to the "shrine" rooms. The excavator observes that where burials are found in "shrines" they are richer in equipment than those in the ordinary houses. Here too are found the ocher burials of females who apparently had some status (only 21 out of some 480 burials).

One of the red ocher burials found in the season of 1965 had cowrie shells placed in the eye sockets to simulate eyes, a common practice in the ancient Near East.[11]

In the so-called hunting shrines discovered in 1965, male burials were not found at all. Instead, women and children in their usual place were all that were found—a provocative situation, since the paintings of the shrine are very much male-oriented with their scenes of the hunt.

Çatal Hüyük is a remarkable revelation of past life, but it tantalizes its interpreters. Enough evidence is available to outline a picture of a way of life of the remote past which should be of great value to those who would trace the prehistoric origins of civilization. There is considerable confusion, however, as the excavators and many of their colleagues claim that the culture achieved by the people of Çatal Hüyük (and their approximate contemporaries at places such as Jericho in Palestine) was civilization itself. Mellaart refers constantly in his writings to Neolithic "civilization" and to Çatal Hüyük as a "town" and even a "Neolithic city." [12] He sets forth the basis of this appellation as "a community with an extensive economic development, specialized crafts, a rich religious life, a surprising attainment in art and an impressive social organization.'' [13] He postulates a town market or bazaar with work-shops, extensive trade, and social stratification and special divisions of the settlement into quarters—one of which at least is ''sacred and residential,'' the whole adding up to ''remains as urban as those of any site from the succeeding Bronze Age yet excavated in Turkey.''

The Population

The evidence put forth to demonstrate that Çatal Hüyük is a city and thus representative of a civilization must be analyzed in the light of the anthropological view of civilization (see Introduction). Critical to that analysis is the relation between a population and its culture. Discovering this relationship takes the form of a detective story. Estimates as to the population of Çatal Hüyük have varied. One method is to work out a running figure for the number of people by comparisons to villages of recent times where the relation of size of house to resident number is known. Mellaart found that the size of the sleeping platforms in the various houses gave a range of from three to eight persons in the rooms in which such platforms were found.[14] One could therefore use a figure of five people per house as a reasonable average estimate—probably two adults and three children, or in other words a nuclear family. Levels VI-A and VI-B—the two levels with the maximum number of rooms revealed in the first three seasons of excavation—contained respectively 25 and 37 rooms, including shrines. This would indicate a population of 125 at level VI-A and 185 at level VI-B for the modernly exposed area. Since this area is regarded as approximately a thirtieth of the whole, simple multiplication reveals populations of 3,750 and 4,550 respectively for levels VI-A and VI-B. Mellaart admits, however, that there is no certainty as to the overall extent of any one level in the site. Furthermore, his postulation of workshops, bazaar, and other public areas within the still unexcavated part of the site would cut heavily into the residential portion, however arranged.

Another hint as to population is obtained from the number of burials recovered. There were 229 burials found in levels VI-A and VI-B combined, representing a time span of 150 years, or approximately six generations. This averages about 38 dead per generation. Since each generation averaged 155 people (in 31 houses), these figures indicate little more than one death per generation per house, much less than one would expect.

Mellaart has pointed out that there is a possible relationship between the number of shrines and the number of ordinary houses, shrines serving houses much perhaps as chapels. The dead of the shrines then belong to the ordinary houses and this would raise the count of those belonging to any house to four to five dead per generation.[15] This is a more likely figure, but it would radically change the number of living quarters, unless the shrines are assumed to have served as living quarters as well. If shrines are excluded, the number of houses at level VI-A is reduced to 12 and the number at VI-B to 11, yielding the following figures (still assuming 5 individuals per house and 30 as the multiple):

Level	Houses	Population of Excavated Area	Population of Total Site
VI-A	12	60	1,800
VI-B	11	55	1,650

Assuming the highest possible number of people per house according to the excavator (i.e. 8), one obtains the following figures:

Level	Houses	Population of Excavated Area	Population of Total Site
VI-A	12	96	2,880
VI-B	11	88	2,640

In other words a revised figure of something less than 3,000 people for the whole population of Çatal Hüyük during what appears to be its heyday seems a more reasonable estimate than the "ten thousand souls" mentioned by Mellaart.[16]

The American physical anthropologist J. L. Angel was able to study 294 individuals of the more than 400 found buried at Çatal Hüyük.[17] His conclusions give vivid insight into the life of the time. Average life expectancy was thirty years for women and thirty-three for men. There is a minimum number of bone fractures resulting from falls—probably from the house ladders or the roofs, and a somewhat higher number of those that indicate warfare or dispute. There is some evidence for a man having been gored—a natural hazard if cattle are to be hunted and herded. The diet was a good one with only occasional lapses. But the daily life meant hard work for everyone, as is evidenced by posture and bone joint stress. Some of the women's teeth are worn, as if they were used for purposes other than chewing food, such as basket weaving or holding the butt of a bowdrill. Angel finds evidence for the mixture of people so that it would appear that a strain of foreign genes was always available to the indigenous pool.

The most striking contribution of Angel's work is the determination of falciparum malaria or its equivalent as a major disease at Çatal Hüyük. This is in keeping with the proximity of swampland, the breeding ground of mosquitoes. There is also evidence that natural selection was at work in developing immunities towards that disease.

Angel has considerable evidence to show that there was a steady population rise at Çatal Hüyük owing to selective factors such as the longer lives of more fecund women. A birthrate of 4.2 children is postulated—meaning that those who survived to age thirty would have given birth to at least four children. The juvenile death rate Angel estimates as four out of every ten deaths. Adult female deaths he feels were largely due to childbirth or the results of childbirth.

Prehistoric Economics

It seems that sometime in the eighth millennium B.C. the low portion of the Konya basin began to emerge, as the lakes which covered it during the last phases of the Pleistocene receded. The exposed land was fertile and well watered, and its vegetation was attractive to the hooved beasts of the temperate region which is much of Anatolia's zoogeographical affinity.[18] The Konya basin offered much natural variety for the adaptation of animal and plant life. The surrounding hills and mountains provided a spectrum of life zones from the alpine to the forested temperate. Marshlands were prevalent at the center of the basin, and streams such as the Carsamba meandered towards and through such low areas extending or diminishing them according to montane rainfall. The general tendency of the climate was towards drier conditions, and thus semiarid zones expanded—especially towards the north, or the plateau. Both on a macro and a micro ecological scale there was a subsistence basis for a great variety of organic life. At least three forms of deer, the ibex, wild ass, pig, auroch, wild ox, gazelle, leopard, lion, fox, weasel, wolf, sheep, goat, bear, rabbit, wildcat, marten, jackel, many marsh birds, and the land tortoise were found in abundance. Fish certainly filled the lakes and streams, and there were freshwater clams as well.

By at least the seventh millennium B.C. this abundance had drawn man the hunter and gatherer to the Konya region. At the foothill site of Suberde west of Çatal Hüyük archaeologists have found a village of prehistoric hunters dating to the time. Their village was located near a lake on a ridge which often is surrounded by the lake waters. Though the site is small, it has yielded a vast number of bones of the animals hunted by the inhabitants. This hunting was carried on with the help of a chipped-stone industry which was 90 percent obsidian. The people lived in smallish huts which, as in Çatal Hüyük, had benches and, at least in a later phase, plastered floors. A figurine or two and some ground-stone objects, the usual bone tools, a bit of pottery and a sliver of copper made up the preserved or identified industry. Sickle blades and grinding stones suggest the possibility of cereal agriculture of some kind. But the subsistence appears to have been predominately that of hunting and gathering, for nearly 300,000 pieces of bone were recovered in situ. Some twenty species of animal were identified, the bulk of which were sheep or goats. The remainder of the animals were largely of the kind familiar at Çatal Hüyük but including land tortoises (*Testudo graecae*) and hedgehogs. Careful analysis of the kinds of bones which represent the basic food animals produced evidence to the effect that wild sheep and goats were cooperatively hunted to such an extent in the earlier years of Suberde's existence that their number declined in the later years— an indication that they were not domesticated. Wild oxen (*Bos primigenius*), whose flesh was apparently succulent but whose behavior was dangerous, were hunted regularly, along with pigs and deer. Wild oxen were to be found at some distance from Suberde and were butchered on the spot in order not to have to carry the whole animal back. For a large animal such as the ox the hunters also worked in groups.[19]

Suberde's hunters were probably typical of the life of the times. Hunting was optimum and a modicum of other subsistence stability was otherwise available in the growth of cereal grains whether wild or not. In addition, the abundance and variety of plants made supplements to the vegetable diet perfectly possible. There is strangely little evidence for fish and birds in spite of the nearby lakes and streams, but then their remains are notoriously fragile.

Assuming that human dietary needs have not changed fundamentally since prehistoric times, a hunter's family (two adults, three adolescent children) living in a temperate climate but involved in hard physical labor would need a minimum of 15,000 calories a day and 400 grams of protein. Meat is generally rich in protein but low in carbohydrates. The cereal grains, fruits, and vegetables are high in carbohydrates and vary a great deal in protein content. A balanced diet occurs when there is an intake from both plant and animal resources. As has been demonstrated in Deh Luran and at other sites, man gathers whatever he knows is edible. The archaeological record at Suberde does not reveal the number and kind of plants, nuts, herbs, cereal grasses, and the like which were the goals of the day's gathering activity, but this unknown but naturally present resource provided the food values which meat alone could not furnish.

It was the collectively oriented hunter-gatherer-cultivator already evidenced at Suberde who settled in the center of the Konya plain. Here was a plant and animal habitat far superior to places such as Suberde. The land was and is very fertile, and thus the successful cultivation of the cereal grains was insured. Moreover, and certainly of equal if not greater appeal, was the abundance of game to be found in what then must have been a grassy parkland. If cattle domestication was part of the subsistence resource control, the boundaries set by the numerous branches of the deltaic Carsamba River were natural enclosures. So, too, for sheep and goats. (The evidence for domestication of any kind at Çatal Hüyük is still uncertain, but Mellaart and others are convinced that it existed.) The remains of wolves, foxes, and leopards suggest that these predators were a constant threat.

A major contrast between Suberde and Çatal Hüyük is in the nature of the artifact repertoire. Çatal Hüyük was clay oriented; furthermore its stone tools and weapons tended to be larger than those of Suberde, though both used obsidian widely. This is a reflection of the differences in physical situation, of course, but in the case of weapons and tools, at least, it evidences other demands and adaptations to those demands.

Until the lower levels of the east mound at Çatal Hüyük are explored there will be no evidence as to whether or not the inhabitants arrived at the site culturally full-blown—that is, whether the assemblage of artifacts and techniques which represent them in the upper levels was already in their possession when they settled at Çatal Hüyük. So far there is no indication of an important evolutionary trend based on the evidence from the already excavated levels. Indeed it is highly improbable that the culture evolved at a single place. It is more likely a summation on the one side of all the cultural accomplishments and traditions of the Konya region

and on the other side an integrated culture with its own uniquenesses.

Aside from the age-old traditions of stone chipping and grinding which has been the marker of prehistoric man, Çatal Hüyük
offers evidence of another equally important technological tradition, that of woodworking, certainly as old as stoneworking. The
use of squared timber in the houses and the carving of wooden
vessels, some of which appear to be prototypes for pottery forms,
was certainly well established by the inhabitants. It suggests the
possibility that their origins were in more wooded country, perhaps
the forested hills to the south or west of the Konya plains.

It has been pointed out that the cultivation of cereal grains
found at Çatal Hüyük could not have originated there. The native
home of the wild forms of emmer and einkorn was elsewhere in
the foothill country of the Near East generally. By the time of the
preserved settlement of Çatal Hüyük, however, these wild forms
were already domesticated. A sure sign of domestication is the
ability of man to move a plant form from its natural ecological
niche to another niche normally foreign or indeed even inimical to
it. Man through artificial selection encourages the growth of strains
which adapt to the new location. Obviously the cereal plants of
Çatal Hüyük flourished. They might be labeled the end product of
a process of plant domestication begun by man perhaps a thousand
years before. This suggests that the settlers of Çatal Hüyük did not
come from a region too different from their eventual location.
Since cereal growing was an essential part of their subsistence, that
process set certain requirements that had to be met. Climate,
water, and soil had to be favorable for cereal cultivation. The combination of good hunting and good soil was the desideratum for early
food-producing man and sets him apart from his Paleolithic ancestors whose food-gathering successes depended on the availability
of what was huntable and gatherable almost solely. It certainly
places him apart from his descendants of the later food-producing
stage where the good soil-water requisite was almost the only
requirement for settlement.

The settlers of Çatal Hüyük had, then, a double requirement, and this requirement was amply fulfilled at the site they chose. How amply is demonstrated not only by the size of Çatal Hüyük East but by the fact that for over a thousand years men flourished there and found no reason to move away. It cannot be emphasized enough that primitive man flourishes where there are optimum conditions. Ethnology testifies to the successes of tribal people who on the basis of optimum hunting-gathering-cultivation conditions either all together or separately were able to develop relatively complex cultural forms and sizable populations. Such fruitions are neither the achievement nor the result of the cultural phenomenon known as civilization.

Why Did They Live by a Swamp?

Çatal Hüyük was situated on the lowest dry soil level before swamp conditions—in other words in the midst of the most watered alluvial or fluvial soils. It will not be surprising if the lowest levels of the site reveal signs of flooding and evidence that the early inhabitants used platforming to raise their houses above waters which rose annually, often creating flood conditions. Whether or not that evidence will be found, there is the lucid fact that nearness to marshland was a desideratum and that people remained there in spite of the mosquito and attendant pests. (Mellaart has noted that so far no wells have been found at Çatal Hüyük. This may be because water was readily accessible in *ponds* nearby.) Lacking knowledge of irrigation and of fertilization, they depended on the muddy alluvial belts and fan plains with their natural moisture and renewed fertility for primitive cultivation. This cultivation most probably involved annual planting by dropping seed in a dibble hole, but the evidence for hoes and for woodworking suggests that a man-drawn plow or a plow adze might have been used.

The locale of the site, then, is evidence that agriculture was of great importance to the inhabitants of Çatal Hüyük; it was obviously chosen deliberately for its cultivation advantages. Only 5 or 6 miles to the south there is a general land rise of some 30 feet—a drier and perhaps more satisfactory living place but a place not sufficiently dependable for the necessary annual crop.

Yet why not live in a drier place and simply walk to the fields? One reason is obviously that a daily walk to fields 3 to 5 miles away would involve some two hours of time. Another is that filled baskets of grain are heavy, and work is much lightened when farmers live in the midst of their fields.

A third reason is vigilance. The animals of the ancient parkland were largely grazers and browsers for whom a wheat field would be of considerable attraction. Birds are notorious grain eaters, as are numerous rodents. The domesticated dog must have been of considerable help in the case of the grazers and browsers but certainly not sufficient to prevent the incursion of hungry animals who by number and appetite could speedily demolish a year's crops. Men had to be on the scene to maintain a watch. With leopards and wolves in the offing that watch could hardly have been the job for a lone sentinel.

But the attraction of the grain fields to the ungulates and their predators was certainly not entirely negative—not when meat was a substantial part of the diet, and skin, bone, and tusk important to the technology. The popular image of prehistoric hunters moving far afield after their prey is probably erroneous in a situation like that of Çatal Hüyük. Man's presence is not necessarily a matter of detraction to many animals. In fact, one can readily assume that a kind of symbiotic relationship existed, in which man inadvertently exchanged a part of his grain yield and perhaps deliberately most of the accompanying straw to attract the animals upon which he fed. Thus the animals obtained a degree of dependent subsistence in exchange for a part of their population. Accompanying benefits such as the manuring of the stubble fields or population control made the relationship all the more valid. The mural paintings and modelings of Çatal Hüyük with their emphasis upon animal life and in particular cattle, deer, and sheep are noteworthy in their lack of scenes of deliberately killed animals—and in this they differ from the cave paintings of Western Europe. At Çatal Hüyük there were hunts, certainly, but the pictures of men waving their arms and dancing about the animals as if to frighten or to impress them suggests more than mere hunting.

Among the graves found at Çatal Hüyük was one of an adult female with mouse bones (*Mus musculus*) apparently deliberately placed with the dead.[20] The reason for this association is unknown, but the notorious love of mice for grain and the association of women with agriculture as demonstrated by the placement of some of the figurines make this combination far from bizarre. It is the clear evidence for mice that should be noted as another example of the relationship of agriculturally inclined man to the animal world at this time. Mice drawn by the stores of grain in each house must have been a constant pest. Weasels, jackals, foxes, wolves, cranes (or storks), and even leopards are naturally attracted by mouse populations of scale. It is unusual that snakes are only depicted here and there in the site (on dagger handles, for example), since cobras, rat snakes, vipers, pythons, and other snakes feed on mice and have a natural home in marshlands and their margins.

The point to be emphasized here is that the agricultural activities of man of the kind postulated for Çatal Hüyük in its almost millennium of existence were attractive to most of the indigenous animals in one way or another. Rather than diminishing man's hunting potential, agriculture probably enhanced it. It is in this kind of situation that the grounds for animal domestication are laid. Both animal domestication and agriculture are evidenced for the later levels at Çatal Hüyük and there is a diminution in both animal and weapon size.[21] The achievement of animal domestication and the expansion of agricultural and grazing land spelled the end of hunting as a major source of food. Whereas the archaeological surveyors of the Konya plain were able to locate only one or two sites contemporary with Çatal Hüyük East, the full-fledged sedentary life of Çatal Hüyük West is evidenced by many sites, obviously necessitating the end of the large game herds which had once roamed there.

One of the frustrating parts of archaeological research of the kind carried on by Mellaart and his colleagues is the fact that erosion and soil accumulation for one reason or another—man or nature—has destroyed or covered over much of the ancient evidences for settlement. Was the great site of Çatal Hüyük at the hub of a settlement pattern with numerous small villages and camps situated about like satellites? Did people live the year round at Çatal Hüyük or disperse to higher ground seasonally? It is of course unlikely that Çatal Hüyük was the only site of the time—but it was more than likely the largest.

James Mellaart refers to Çatal Hüyük as a civilization, emphasizing the complexity of the culture there as indicated by the numerous occupations evidenced. He even goes so far as to expect to find special areas on the site devoted to one or another of these occupations.[22] He implies that this multiplicity of occupation and its dependent materials represent urban wealth which has as its basis "a well-organized trade" with obsidian at its heart. Although the elaborate technological organization, capital, and commerce are all essentials of civilization at one level, the culture at Çatal Hüyük is more truly representative of the cultural form summarized in the terms *tribal* and *chieftainship*.

The basis of this contention is set forth on the diagrammatic map of Çatal Hüyük and its vicinity (page 168) and in Tables 4 and 5. Of the twenty occupations represented at Çatal Hüyük which can be defined from the combination of materials used and the processes necessary to turn them into usable artifacts, there are none that do not fall within the normal capabilities of the various members of tribes found in various parts of the world. Sex and age division of labor, lulls in subsistence activity, and the support of certain skilled members of the group on an individual basis make possible the elaborations in cultural style among some known groups which are on a par and indeed superior to that of Çatal Hüyük—all in an "uncivilized" context.

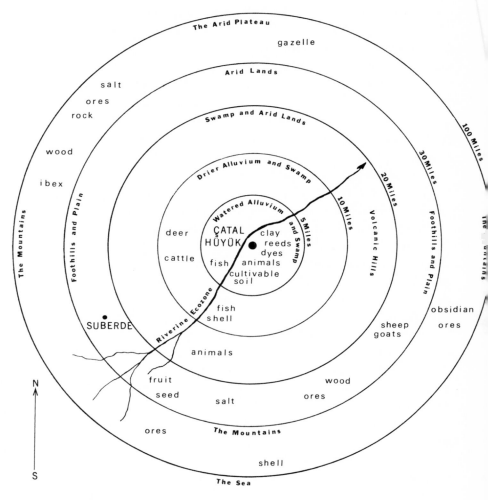

Çatal Hüyük and Vicinity

Nor are these processes beyond the normal technological talents of the home group. Though craftsmen such as carpenters, bead makers, and basket weavers may be labeled and set apart, it has been shown from innumerable examples that individuals so labeled perform many different tasks and control many technological processes in the cycle of the year. The Konyak Naga, for example, manufacture almost everything they use in the home village. Ornaments are traded from village to village, and the products of an especially skilled individual in any craft are valued and traded. Metallurgy is also a domestic activity, with one village perhaps outspurring the others owing to access, to raw material, or to craft tradition.[23] Furthermore, the evidence for such a technological tradition at Çatal Hüyük is feeble. Open-fire roasting of galena to produce lead and the cold hammering of native copper are not always the special province of a group of individuals whose labors are paid for in goods and services. Both these techniques are well within the abilities of the man of the village.[24]

The hypothesis that Çatal Hüyük was a trade center has to be qualified by the rather formidable evidence that its physical situation was due to favorable advantages in hunting-gathering and cultivation. As the diagrammatic map shows, much of the raw material upon which the local technology depended was obtainable within 20 miles of the site. Furthermore, all the artifacts identified at Çatal Hüyük (table 5) were to be found no more than 100 miles away. Again it is a misconception of the mobility of primitive man to assume that because some of the important raw materials upon which he depended were far afield he traded with others to obtain them. This he may well have done, but he could equally as well have gone to get them himself. Obsidian, for example, was obtainable within 100 miles of Çatal Hüyük.[25] It is of interest that there is no indication at Çatal Hüyük that objects were manufactured from obsidian there. Indeed, why carry raw material so far from its source? More than likely much of the obsidian tool manufacture was carried out at the source, thus lessening carrying weight, whether portage was by a trader or a commuting citizen. A further problem is to identify what was traded: on the one side, obsidian; on the other, leopard skins, dyes, carved wood? None of these commodities was confined to the Çatal Hüyük area.

Again it must be emphasized that for the entire 800 years postulated for its existence Çatal Hüyük East was a place of stability. There is no evidence for abandonment even though there was a

conflagration or two and malaria took its toll. Commerce is a notoriously uncertain foundation, and Çatal Hüyük's stability is lucid
evidence that its economic basis was secure.

Social Organization

The most telling indication of Çatal Hüyük's cultural status is
the evidence for social and political organization. Nothing so far
found at Çatal Hüyük can be regarded as a purely public structure
such as a fort, temple, or palace. Mellaart, on the basis of murals,
reliefs, and special graves, identifies the area he has been excavat-
ing as the priestly quarter and suggests other quarters of the site for
other ranks and occupations.[26] If one assumes a priesthood and
other such special social stations, one must also assume an ad-
ministrative apparatus. A population of 3,000 (or, if Mellaart's
own estimate is correct, 5,000), particularly if it is divided by occupation and social status, needs overall controls to make it function. As the American anthropologist Robert L. Carneiro has
shown, there is a direct correlation between population size and
social complexity: "If a society does increase significantly in size,
and if at the same time it remains unified and integrated, it must
elaborate its organization." [27]

A priesthood can be regarded as an organizational trait responsive to the increased complexity of religious practice and thus the
result of adaptations—to the need for organization made necessary
by increased population, and to the need for direction in the face
of changing ideas as to religious belief. Although there is some evidence for population growth at Çatal Hüyük, and although the
evidence for a shift towards an increasing dependence on agriculture indicates that changes in ritual beliefs concerning hunting and
agriculture were underway,[28] there is no indication that population
significantly differed from the lowest to the highest levels known
at the site nor that there was important change in ideology. Moreover, the presence of religious art and the practice of burial with
grave goods does not necessarily involve a priesthood.

Society and Polity

Although it is unlikely that the society of Çatal Hüyük was complex enough to be regarded as a full-fledged civilization, there is evidence for some social and political organization.

First, there is good evidence for a sexual division of labor. The grave goods demonstrate that women were responsible for basketry, objects of personal adornment, cosmetic grinding and use, cooking and other household tasks, and very likely horticulture. From the fact that basket-weaving tools are found with Çatal Hüyük women and that women generally do the weaving in primitive societies, the spinning and weaving of textiles were very likely women's tasks. Men were the hunters and warriors, the reapers of grain, the cutters and the carvers of wood. It can be assumed that men chipped and ground their own stone for tools and weapons, made their own bows and arrows, built the houses, and made any journeys that may have been necessary to obtain distant raw materials.

Second, the houses, though varied in size, are contiguous and the whole settlement aspect is communal. This and the lack of evidence for rich and poor suggests strongly that the society was egalitarian rather than structured into classes or hierarchies. The nature of the art found at Çatal Hüyük supports this view. Several exploratory studies of the role of art as an expression of social condition have been made by sociologists, psychologists, anthropologists, and art historians.[29] The American anthropologist John L. Fischer, for example, has created a model based on the idea that society breaks down into two ideal types: hierarchical and egalitarian. On a scale these ideal types would represent opposite poles. The artist as a member of his society is directly subject to its social values, and his graphic expression of them is subject to two main conditions: the spectrum of possibilities which the society permits him to use or will respond to, and his own subconscious and conscious response to the social condition in which he lives. In this regard the excavator of Çatal Hüyük has noted that there is variance of artistic execution at the site—good work and bad work—as well as different "styles"—even in the same composition.[30] Furthermore, there is a degree of spontaneity about the paintings, not found as frequently in the reliefs. Apparently no effort was made to compose the scene before its execution.[31] All this suggests that the conditions for mural painting were not formalized—that there was no specific school or guild of special artists.

Fischer's scale analysis of works of art as related to types of society (authoritarian to egalitarian) was based on data provided by George P. Murdock and Herbert Barry. It draws upon data from some twenty-nine societies throughout the world:

> If we assume that pictorial elements in design are, on one psychological level, abstract, mainly unconscious representations of persons in the society, we may deduce a number of hypothetical polar contrasts in art style:
>
> (1) Design repetitive of a number of rather simple elements should characterize the egalitarian societies; design integrating a number of unlike elements should be characteristic of the hierarchical societies.
>
> (2) Design with a large amount of empty or irrelevant space should characterize the egalitarian societies; design with little irrelevant (empty) space should characterize the hierarchical societies.
>
> (3) Symmetrical design (a special case of repetition) should characterize the egalitarian societies; asymmetrical design should characterize the hierarchical societies.
>
> (4) Figures without enclosures should characterize the egalitarian societies; enclosed figures should characterize the hierarchical societies.[32]

If these criteria are applied to the murals of Çatal Hüyük, the result is to place Çatal Hüyük's society nearer to the egalitarian pole than to the authoritarian. Admitting that this kind of interpretation is open to hard questioning, it nonetheless has its value in that it is not contradictory to the idea of community given by other evidence.

A third factor bearing upon the social character of Çatal Hüyük is the relationship of population size to complexity of social organization.[33] As population grows, there is an increasing need for organization to preserve the society's cohesion. In single community societies, according to Robert L. Carneiro, "the number of organizational traits . . . is equal (roughly) to the square root of the population." [34] Postulating a population of two to three thousand at Çatal Hüyük (rather than the excavator's own estimate of five thousand), the society would exhibit sixty to a hundred organizational traits by Carneiro's scale. Societies comparable to Çatal Hüyük on this scale are the Maori, the Rewala, Bedouin, the Acoma Pueblo Indians, and the Batak of Sumatra, all of which qualify as chieftainships. The chieftainship is a directional organization of society around a leader whose rank is permanent or can be permanent and whose office involves certain obligations such as leadership in war. Important to the office, whether implicit or explicit, is the role of the chief as one who redistributes goods from the producer to the consumer.[35]

In connection with leadership at Çatal Hüyük there are several hints, the most obvious being the scenes of human beings represented in the murals. Mellaart's discovery of the so-called hunting shrines in the season of 1965 has added considerably to knowledge of the life of the times. On the southern end of the west wall some fifteen bearded men wearing dark loincloths cavort about a great red stag which by its leg position and the fact that its tail and tongue (?) are being pulled about is obviously recently dead. Two lesser figures of children (?), a steatopygous woman, and a dog watch the scene. It is a lively and almost comical one, with the men energetically moving about the animal pulling and pushing in a ludicrous manner. Of the bearded men none seems to carry weapons, though a knife or two may be worn in the belt of some. About half the men wear leopard-skin pelts or parts of pelts at their waists. Of these only about three have tails attached.

On the same wall but at the north end two stags (?), a boar, two wild asses, and what appears to be a dog are the central elements of another kind of scene. The stags appear to be dead, while the boar, very much alive, is challenged by two lively figures bearing nets but otherwise featureless. The asses may be running; one of them is apparently being chased by a man while the other is apparently being held at the muzzle, suggesting that the animal is either dead or pacified. The first ass also has a figure close to its snout. The asses are being "watched" by a headless figure who sits legs apart, an elbow on one knee and a hand on the other.

Beyond and above the animals generally is a rather stately group of men, most of whom stand upright, pointing with bows or curbed sticks at the stags. Three, however, leap about close to the animals. Two of these are apparently naked. Most of the remaining men wear what appears to be the conventional leopard skin at the waist. Most of the men have both arms raised at the elbow. A single figure at the top of the composition appears to be lying down but not dead. A line of what appear to be women inclines from the midst of this scene into the next, joining both into a whole.

The next scene is the most dramatic in the "shrine." A great bull apparently very much alive is surrounded by some thirty-odd people, mostly men. Below him wild asses move across the landscape. All the figures are in monochrome (reds) except for one above the bull and the group directly in front of him. The first figure has half his body painted white (or pink). One of the vigorously moving figures before the bull is more elaborately dressed than the others. He wears a leopard-skin cap and skirt, the latter decorated with tassels or bull or other animal tails. He stands weaponless, close to the animal's horns, waving his arms. Around him, others dressed almost as elaborately vigorously move about waving bows, throwing sticks (?), and apparently having trouble keeping their skins on.

Behind the bull a group of rather featureless men and boys gesture vigorously at the bull; they are led by a polychrome figure whose appearance suggests body painting, perhaps with pipe clay. One small and youthful figure has apparently leaped onto the back of the bull while another prods him with a bow below. Women and children, including a steatopygous female, watch the scene.

On the east end of the north wall there is a scene like that of the south end of the west wall in which an apparently dead stag is pushed and pulled by a group of mostly leopard-skin-clad figures, two of whom are painted whitish or pink. Another group runs about an angry boar.

This scene links up with another, on the east wall, where another boar and a bear are equally beset by running figures that are if anything the liveliest of the whole shrine.

Their sinuous liveliness contrasts with another group of upright, apparently dancing, figures centered on an elaborately skirted main figure who holds one hand on his hip and waves the other. A third and lower row of these dancers has been largely eliminated.

A final scene of the east wall is found at its southern end, where a group of dancing (?) figures circles about what may be a lion.

The south wall murals are poorly preserved, but enough remains to evidence that the wild ass, cranes (or storks) and boars were important parts of the scene.

A tantalizing scene of what appears to be a large kneeling figure with a mane of hair confronted by curving, bent-over figures, one of whom lies prone, was found at the east end of this south wall. The scene is terminated by a seated female, legs wide apart, her right arm on her head.

Another "hunting shrine," found on level III, was not nearly so well preserved as that on level V, but sufficient remained to indicate that its subject matter was essentially the same—men and animals—and the vigor of the scene is identical. The stags here, however, are being hunted. One of the figures strikes a drum—the only representation of this instrument so far found.

Several salient features of these scenes are indicative of the social system:

- The active people are the men; women are largely onlookers.
- There are three distinct groups of men: the bearded loinclothed group, the leopard-skin-clad group, and the featureless group who appear in monochrome; among these there appear to be children and acrobats. (Mellaart has noted figures without heads—but in view of the state of preservation of these murals it is not certain that these should be regarded as a separate category.)
- There are figures whose bodies are painted.
- Though there is considerable weaponry depicted, the figures nearest to a dangerous animal seldom carry weapons. Such figures seem to be more elaborately costumed than others.
- There is definite evidence for dancing in lines and perhaps in circles.
- There is tremendous vigor in the scenes, especially in the immediate presence of animals.

The ethnological interpretation of this evidence is that there exist societies, clubs, age groups, and clans whose members relate to one another on several bases: common goals in hunting, warfare, or other collective activity; assumed or actual kin relationships through a common ancestor, sometimes designated as a totem. They have initiations, meetings, costumes, yearly rituals, and duties of their own. They can regulate the observance of marriage and other customs and can act as regulators in daily activity. Such groups, called sodalities by anthropologists, are the marker of the tribal level of social organization.[36]

Because these organizations are pantribal they act as cohesive forces in the society. An individual is not only a member of a family but of a group to which he has equally stringent obligations. From such groups comes the collective organization necessary to offset the stresses of the outside world and often to resolve the quarrels within the society. The sodalities require the demonstration by the individual of as near the ideal as possible.

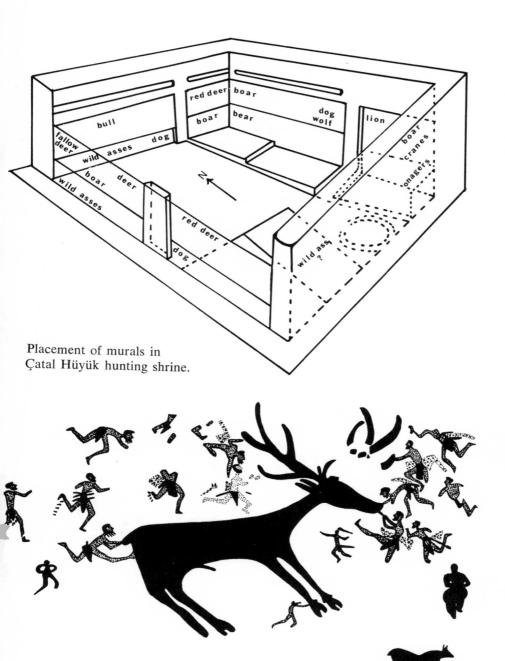

Placement of murals in
Çatal Hüyük hunting shrine.

Stag hunt, west wall of Çatal Hüyük hunting shrine.

Boar and other animals, west wall of Çatal Hüyük hunting shrine.

The great bull, north wall of Çatal Hüyük hunting shrine.

Stag hunt, north wall of Çatal Hüyük hunting shrine.

Boar and bear, east wall of Çatal Hüyük hunting shrine.

Lion (?), east wall of Çatal Hüyük hunting shrine.

The evidence for groups of men at least two of which are clearly different in costume and appearance and yet not antagonistic to one another suggests social differentiation. Moreover, the elaborately clad or painted individuals who weaponless toy with animals at bay evidence that there were leaders who by their prowess had rank to which their courage and skill entitled them. Their rank, however, seems to have been only within the special group such as the leopard-skin-clad men. Body painting and dancing are ceremonial attributes of ritual and the use of certain colors for the former and participation right in the latter are common elements of in-group membership.

Were the leopard-skin people a clan? If so, it may be that the "shrines" in which leopard reliefs and modeled forms appear are clan chambers like the kivas of the American Southwest. Perhaps there were bull clans and stag clans, in accordance with dominant symbols. Perhaps those without the leopard skins are commoners or novitiates and therefore unable to wear the symbols of the clan whose totemic ancestor was the leopard. This is speculation, of course, yet it is clear from the murals that sodalities were prevalent at Çatal Hüyük.

The absence of women's active participation in the main events depicted is certainly a clear indication of women's place in hunting activity. It is important, therefore, to note Mellaart's observation that only women were buried in these "hunting shrines." [37] It is difficult, however, to relate these vigorous scenes with all their spontaneity to ritual expressions. One is inclined to view them more as the kind of paintings one finds at sports clubs. There is a zest and spirit in the paintings that belies any serious cultistic reference. Its very secularity points to the kind of sodality which, based upon empiricism, nonetheless gains for its members a natural mystique to which all pay obeisance without sacred allusion. The kind of burial found designates membership of the individual and it is probable that, as in many clans or societies, one's wife was given a particular status—especially if the husband was an outstanding individual.

There is strong evidence, then, that the social organization of Çatal Hüyük was characterized by a clear-cut sexual division of labor, an egalitarian communal life, the presence of sodalities (some of which were for men but gave status to women and were centered around hunting), and leadership in the hands of chiefs— presumably the leaders of particular sodalities whose special functions could be called into play according to the needs which they best served or for which they had been created. These characteristics present a picture strikingly similar to that of a chiefdom as described by M. D. Sahlins in *Tribesmen:*

> A chiefdom is not a class society. Although a stage beyond primitive equalitarianism, it is not divided into a ruling stratum in command of the strategic means of production or political coercion and a disenfranchised underclass. It is a structure of degrees of interest rather than conflicts of interest: of graded familial priorities in the control of wealth and force, in claims to others' services, in access to divine power, and in material styles of life—such that, if all the people are kinsmen and members of society, still some are more members than others. [38]

Relations with the Outside World

At the time of Çatal Hüyük's heyday, there were a great number of settlements to be found in the Konya plain, although no one knows just how many. In any case there is little question that Çatal Hüyük was in a dominant position in the center of the great plain. Ancient village sites outside the plain, such as Suberde to the southwest, Asikli Hüyük to the northeast,[39] Can Hasan to the south, Erbaba and perhaps Hacilar to the west, and even Mersin near the coast to the southeast are suggestive of varying ways of life whose longevity and contemporaneity are still being determined. In any case there is strong evidence that in the seventh millennium B.C. within a given region, such as that of Konya, there were adaptations to given ecological niches which had their own cultural characteristics. Subsistence obtainment emphases differed from complete hunting-gathering to almost total food production. The heterogeneity of the Çatal Hüyük population is proof of differing physical strains intermingling in the plain.[40] (Archaeologists would be hard put to recover the material evidence for the campsites of bands that more than likely moved seasonally from one place to the next dependent on tradition and success in finding food.)

To say that men of differing backgrounds and interests were always peaceable to one another would be a denial of history. Furthermore, even though the men's daily labors undeniably kept them busy, it is difficult to envision any group of young males living without the need for physical challenge. If a fifth of the population were adult males, then in a population of 3,000 there would be 600 males presumably fit for offense as well as defense. The mural scenes show an exuberant crowd of men zestfully enjoying the hunt, and the results of the hunt, even to the extent of baiting a dangerous beast. Angel has determined that a number of his skeletons exhibit marks of blows. Furthermore, the depiction of leop-

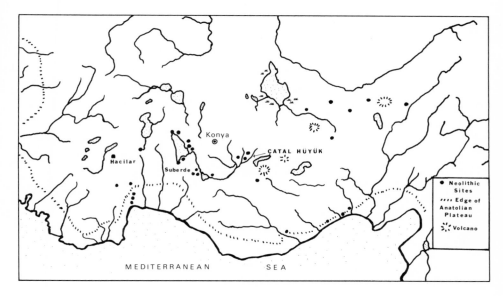

Early Sites in Anatolia

ard, bull, boar, ram, and stag in mural and relief indicate they were given value both for their own sakes and for their relationship to men. One can almost hear such expressions as "brave as a bull," "fierce as a leopard," or "majestic as a stag" as labels of male behavior.

It is probable that men fought one another as always. Mellaart indeed feels that the doorless houses with roof entrances only were excellent for defense. Çatal Hüyük may well have been under some stress because its permanent situation in the midst of the plain made it a target for attack by roving bands seeking the fruit of field and home. (Conflagration is attested at Çatal Hüyük, though it is by no means certain it was caused by enemies.) Warfare was probably of the quick raid and counterraid type so prevalent among primitive people. Warfare in such cases is carried out by given groups of men organized in clans or clubs, in which considerable prestige is given to the successful conqueror of the enemy. In such cases prisoner taking is often regarded as the material mark of success, and the disposal of prisoners of war through ritual execution, head removal, or sacrifice is common. Some of the burials in the shrines of Çatal Hüyük could conceivably have been of such prisoners. To bury in one's home the body of a brave antagonist or of a brave enemy's relative gives prestige to the house owner's family.

Warfare, however waged, requires organization, and this appears to have been a factor in the cohesiveness of Çatal Hüyük; so does large-scale hunting. Such hunting has been suggested for Suberde, and is certainly as ancient as the Upper Paleolithic.

Mellaart has observed that organization is prevalent everywhere on the site. This does not necessarily mean that there was a class or a body of individuals dictating certain ways of doing things. Rather it bespeaks of tradition—the historical assurance of the group's validity. "These ways of doing things have always worked." The building of houses is society's responsibility even though individual specialists may be called in to square timbers, orient corners, or plaster walls. Such specialists develop as part of the reaction of society to daily needs as well as to the traditional ways. Some individuals can do things better than others—sometimes because of native talent, sometimes because of training—but always within the boundaries set forth by the tradition. In the modern world skills are valued as innovative rather than traditional. "Better ways of doing things" is a chapter heading in a popular social science text, and indeed such slogans are the basis of the enterprise of many an industrial firm. Organization was evidenced at all levels at Çatal Hüyük, underlining the cohesiveness of the ancient society and its basis in tradition—another precious piece of evidence in the reconstruction of a past way of life.

When there is evidence for strong tradition in one part of a culture, there is little reason to deny the role of tradition in other parts. This principle emphasizes the overall unity which enabled Çatal Hüyük to flourish over many centuries, but it also denies that that unity was maintained by arbitrary rulership. Whatever the outside stresses which required leadership, there is nothing in the archaeological record to suggest that that leadership had its own growth, became institutionalized, and ultimately changed the character of the social organization. Nor is there any indication of a rise and fall of prosperity, periods of florescence and periods of economic falling-off due to military and political aggrandizement and degrandizement. Çatal Hüyük seems to have been marked by stable prosperity. Strong workable traditions of technology, economics, social organization, and polity were there and enabled the inhabitants to offset human enemies and natural problems of disease, climate, and subsistence.

Religious Beliefs

A cultural area often misconstrued is that of belief, in particular religious belief. There is evidence that the people of Çatal Hüyük embraced animism, the belief that the world, material and immaterial, is under the control of the supernatural. Much has been written about the fact that primitive man is in the midst of the animistic world and is a part of it. His conceptions are owing to his place within it, not because of his own ability to stand outside and analyze it objectively.[41] Mellaart, after reviewing the reliefs, paintings, figurines, statues, and burial customs of Çatal Hüyük, has set forth the concept of a pantheon.[42] The supreme deity is the "Great Goddess" who has a bearded husband, a daughter, and a son: the "holy family." These in sum are really aspects of certain basic themes, "the whole aim of the religion being to ensure the continuity of life in every aspect: wildlife for the hunter, domesticated life for the civilized communities and finally the life of Neolithic man himself." [43] He refers of course to certain rooms as "shrines" and has, by referring to both the placement and the symbolism of murals, reliefs, and modeled animal heads, constructed a plausible iconographic picture. He has found evidence for food and artifact offerings but no blood sacrifices. Even the plastering over of wall paintings has religious significance, for those paintings are regarded as having been "created for religious occasions." Burial rites in which the color black meant death and red meant life are suggested, and cultism of various kinds is pointed out. Mellaart goes so far as to hypothesize a religious class of priests and priestesses who administer this religion—and to whose quarters the chance of excavation has led the British team.

Most striking of the customs revealed by the evidence from Çatal Hüyük are the burials. As indicated previously, burial was secondary; that is, upon death the individual corpse was buried— or very probably exposed (as the vulture murals indicate)—until most of the flesh was removed from the bones. The bones—particularly the skulls—were decorated in some cases, and the whole was then buried under the platforms in the houses, some with extensive funerary furniture and some not, but most with food offerings. There was more elaborate burial for some than for others, probably indicative of their value to the society.

Examples of this kind of funerary custom have been found among numerous primitive people.[44] The custom has many variations, but there is one universal theme—that the spirits of the dead must in some way be recognized, cared for, or launched on their way. There were four stages of the funerary rite:

1. *Time of death.* The corpse was moved to its temporary interment. This was the most difficult period for the living community. The impact of loss on relatives and friends had to be reduced through rituals of mourning. The corpse had to be treated and moved in accordance with custom which involved such matters as sex and age of the individual, as well perhaps as a concern for social status. In any case separation of the corpse from the living community is explicit. A sense of danger may have been involved in this procedure, for the cause of death and the new corpse are closely related.

2. *Period of transition.* Much seems to have been made of this time, as is evident from the vulture murals. The body exposed to the air was defleshed by eaters of carrion and thus converted into a skeleton—the enduring part of the physical body. Apparently the brain was preserved, for Mellaart reports that numerous skulls still

contained the remains of brains, and in one case where the brain was absent a ball of fine cloth was substituted.[45] Presumably this was a period of mourning for the family, expressed in unknown ways but possibly involving taboos on certain foods, activities, and social contacts. Some primitive groups believe the spirit of the deceased is freed only when the flesh is gone. As the dead are converted from their living semblance to the skeletal form, so the harmful factors that brought their death in the first place are eaten away and what is left is enduring. The bones represent the freed spirit and can bring luck.

3. *House burial*. The return of the deceased to the house restored familial unity, and the individuals were buried under the sleeping platforms they had occupied in life—an important consideration in any effort to understand ancient social structure. The equal treatment of both sexes in terms of grave placement in the home argues for a bilateralism with perhaps some tendencies towards an emphasis on the female line.

Vultures and other scavengers were obviously not permitted to scatter the bones of the deceased—the house burials make this fairly clear. The finding of a number of bodiless skulls and the murals of headless men attacked by vultures suggests that the head may have been removed in some cases prior to exposure.

4. *The afterlife*. The discovery of food offerings for all burials and individualistic funerary furniture for some indicates a belief in an afterlife—a spirit world where the individual was as he was in the living world. The food may relate to the needs of the freed spirit on its journey to the underworld or it may be symbolic sustenance—a pledge by the living family to the dead of the recognition of the perpetual interdependence of the living and the dead.

This familial interdependence is clearly evidenced at Çatal Hüyük. The houses were occupied over long periods of time, walls are replastered year after year, and as a house grew too old its structure was dismantled in such a way as to provide a foundation for a new house built almost exactly like the old one. Each rebuild was a reiteration of the familial theme: unity of the living and the dead and continuity of traditional ways.

With an average life expectancy of thirty years and a high death rate, death must have been present on an almost daily basis. Malarial-type disease with its cyclic periods of onset and recession produces in the victim a degree of melancholia in the quiet stages and often delirium in the active. The stress factors of hard work, disease, and high death rate are reflected in the cultural personality of the inhabitants of Çatal Hüyük. A society in which few live past the age of forty is likely to put high value on longevity, with wisdom credited to the surviving elderly. Their counsel, individually or collectively, no doubt was sought from time to time, as occurs in many communities of the world. It seems that both sexes were valued and the loss of any individual was a loss of a unit of the energy which collectively made life for the whole community flourish. Some individuals of both sexes were particularly important because of their social and economic functions, and their death was calamitous—except that their spirits never really left the community. Ritual saw to that through its reinforcement of traditional burial customs and the observance of rites.

Life and death were one and the same process. Women's breasts were modeled and made part of the walls. Breasts are the symbols of life-giving nourishment—yet within these breasts are the jaws of carnivores and the carrion-eating vulture. The unity of existence is symbolized in the statue of the ''goddess'' clutching on each side the heads of leopards—the stealthy death-bringers whose prey was impartially men and animals—while from between her legs appears the head of a child being born. It is significant that the statue was found in the grain bin of one of the houses. Most of the women depicted in statue and painting are steatopygous—big-bellied and big-breasted—obviously expressive of a cultural ideal parallel to that of Dolni Vestonice, that life should be a constant reiteration of the power of birth to match the power of death. Rarely are a couple shown in a sexual embrace, and the sexual organs are never depicted. Sexual love and its relationship to birth were apparently not nearly as important as the birth itself. There seems to have been little or no ritualism as regards sexual relationships.

In societies where there is a relatively clear separation between men's and women's work, the degree of common relationship between the sexes is greatly reduced. Sex for purposes other than reproduction is therefore far less common than in societies where the separation is less sharp. In this kind of social system men and women find their membership in the society in different ways. It is important to note again here that the individual's identity depends upon his social integration within the group. In the woman's case her identity rests with other women as a partner in the carrying out of specific domestic tasks which she has a moral obligation to fulfill. Because of her role as a childbearer and mother, her daily life is geared to the home and to other women and children. The man, on the other hand, finds his identity with other men outside the home. The evidence for the existence of men's sodalities confirms this situation at Çatal Hüyük. The women's social relationships are often kin-based while the men's are non-kin except as the sodality defines nonconsanguinal relations. This has its effect on childrearing in that girls are isolated early from their brothers and have little interaction with their fathers. Their job is to learn from female relatives how to accomplish the duties of the daily routine. For boys, the quicker they can undertake a role in the father's world the better.[46]

Agriculture has perhaps a mitigating effect on the separation of the sexes, for its maintenance produces certain commonalities. The evidence suggests that women cultivated the planted fields and that men reaped them. Time-honored custom throughout the world gives reason to suspect that women prepared the bread by sifting, grinding, and baking. It is not known who actually planted, gathered, and winnowed; perhaps it was a task of the whole family and community, since these tasks are seasonal. The presence of the female statuettes in grain bins and the general absence of female participation in the depicted hunts suggests that agriculture was one of the female-oriented activities.

There is also a suggestion that agriculture, though important, was not an overriding consideration in social relationships. Land is of vital importance in the inheritance pattern of agricultural societies. Where familial land is inherited the number of eligible children (usually male) becomes critical. Fractionalization of family land because of inheritance can be significant, for each unit of the new family receives less than before. This is in many societies the cause of sons moving away from the family to seek new land or other productive work. At Çatal Hüyük the high death rate was certainly a factor in reducing the number of potential inheritors. However, the fact that one house succeeds another year after year, that the occupation of the site is continuous, and that there is little evidence for satellite settlements nearby suggests that individual inheritance of land was not the custom. This reinforces the hypothesis of communal ownership indicated by the tight nucleation of the settlement.

Women's relationship to agriculture, to birth, and to the home can be summarized in the term *stability*. There can be little doubt that a dominant theme in the cosmological consciousness of the prehistoric inhabitants of Çatal Hüyük was the (to us) paradoxical relationship of life and death in the fecund woman. The frequent death of women in childbirth evidenced by the burials may have reinforced this theme.

Prominent in the "shrines" are the modeled heads of bulls with aurochs' horns, painted and repainted, sometimes in proximity to or actually ornamented with painted human hands. The most explicit account of the relationship of the bull to the beliefs of the time is found in rooms where the bull is being born out of the body of a "divine" female. The fecundity of the cattle herd (rams' heads are also numerous in the rooms) is symbolized by relating human and animal birth.

The evidence indicates a world view in which birth and death are conceived as aspects of the same basic theme. Man lives in a stable world of spirit and flesh which requires that all living things move from one existence to another, in each of which one has a moral obligation to carry on one's duties. The constant repainting and plastering over of murals and reliefs emphasizes this continuity. Death is like a plastering over of an old painting; it simply prepares the wall for a new existence exactly like the older existence. It suggests that the spirit world and the physical world had no sharp boundaries between them and that, as in most primitive societies, consciousness of one was possible in the other through dreams, omens, and other phenomena.

The religious practitioner was not representative of a full-time hierarchy but was rather an interpreter of omens and dreams, a curer of illness, and a warder-off of evil—in other words, someone who was more shamanistic than priestly.

Among the figurines found at the site are those of animals who had been deliberately "killed" (as at Dolni Vestonice) and eventually buried in pits. This proclaims the presence of the practice of sympathetic magic in which control over a victim, animal or human, comes about by making an image of the victim and then treating that image as if it were living—for whatever the desired result. Such practices are suggested not only by the animal figures but by the pregnant-woman statues as well. The supernatural powers of the known world are called upon to transfer the magical semblance into the real one: "If I sleep in my father's bed, his body a foot or two below me, we communicate through dreams, but what he tells me may be unintelligible to me without interpretation. Disease is caused by the loss of spirit—return the spirit to the body and health returns, but only certain individuals are capable of finding and bringing the spirit back to the body. If one wears a stone, a piece of wood, or a shell of a certain type on one's person, luck will result or evil will be averted." These are beliefs often found in shamanism, the religious practice based on the ability of individuals to contact or influence the supernatural.

These shamans differ from priests in that they are often part-time only and retain their status only insofar as they can constantly demonstrate their ability to contact the supernatural.

At Çatal Hüyük there is a suggestion that there were supervisors who laid down the general rules which the society was to follow as to building, iconography, and ritual, but there is little in the evidence to indicate a full-scale priesthood. The practices of magic and ritual seem to have been seasonal and impromptu rites dependent on the empirical demands of the day: the planting season, illness, the fertility of the family and the herds and flocks, success in the hunt, protection against bad luck, and the necessary rituals of burial. It may be that these demands were met through the cooperation of a few full-time religious practitioners whose support the collective economy could maintain, but there appears to be no good evidence of a body of priests and priestesses. Neither the deities nor the exigencies of life were such as to require the formalization of a priestly hierarchy.

The Moral Order

One overriding characteristic of primitive societies is the pervading sense of morality in the world. Things do as they are created to do. All creatures, including men, have a moral obligation to do that which their role in society or in nature requires of them. The vulture eats the dead, the leopard stalks his prey, the great bull charges, women bear young, men hunt, people laugh, people die, the seasons change, spirits hunger or cry or talk through dreams, storms rage, vegetation grows. In human society, where there is apparent deviance, there are mythological explanations and there are social sanctions, the most powerful form of which is the "shame" incurred by an individual who is ostracized from the group—the family, clan, or club which gives him his identity, his place in the universe. The sense of mutual obligation is the most cohesive force in primitive society. It sets common standards of behavior which regulate social relations among the living, among the dead, and between the living and the dead. These obligations are largely understood and not stated. They are learned as the life of the society proceeds. Out of them comes the ideas of right and wrong, of punishment and reward, of success and failure. So long as this moral cohesiveness is dominant in a society, so long will that society remain an effective unity. At Çatal Hüyük the long continuum of traditional life and the physical scale of the prehistoric village are evidence that the moral order was a strong one and that the accepted practices were workable, whether they related to the struggle for subsistence, the values of social relationships, or the impact of the outside world. This impression is at variance with the idea that a priesthood regulated religious affairs in a society of special practitioners, traders, and craftsmen. The interdependencies set up by such groups require more explicit controls than the traditional moral order of primitive people precipitates. These controls necessarily require constant adjustment as the relationships between groups change. The moral order which binds priests to priests differs from that which binds commoner to commoner, and these differences in moral obligation open gaps between individuals for their standards differ. What compels a man to support a priesthood in a simple system of an exchange of goods for services may be a sense of moral obligation. What keeps a priesthood in power as it proliferates would be increasingly coercive with the compulsion of an individual to give up a part of his produce in exchange for religious services wanted or unwanted. There is nothing in the evidence so far unearthed at Çatal Hüyük to demonstrate anything else than a cohesive and flourishing mutuality of the kind found wherever primitive man has flourished.[47] The history of institutionalized specialists in the larger society is one demonstrating readjustment and change within comparatively short periods of time, and there is no evidence for that history at Çatal Hüyük. What is evidenced is a common affirmation of the same way of life over a long period of time in spite of stress, an affirmation consistent with the moral order as primitive man has known it.

Economics

According to James Mellaart, the excavator of Çatal Hüyük, "One cannot possibly be wrong in suggesting that it was a well-organized trade that produced the city's wealth." [48] He then identifies the obsidian trade as "at the heart of this extensive commerce." The possibility that the polity of Çatal Hüyük might be that of a chiefdom raises the questions of the character of the economic system. Manning Nash, an American anthropologist, in his stimulating study of primitive and peasant economic systems, has identified the four different kinds of exchange systems: mobilization, in which an elite gathers and controls goods and services for the good of the society; markets, the kind of exchange by which goods are traded on the basis of maximum return to seller and buyer; reciprocal exchange, the equivalence giving of goods and services, which often involves the prestige of the individual, his family, or clan; and the redistributive system, "a form of reciprocity with political or economic centricity. Some central agency collects goods or commands services and then distributes them among the social units and persons who have professed them."

He further goes on to suggest a developmental line for these systems: "Except for mobilization exchange, there is a suggested developmental career for exchange systems: from reciprocity to redistribution to market." [49]

The evidence at Çatal Hüyük indicates an egalitarian character. This egalitarianism is a function of a communal way of life in which the family is the basic productive unit. Collective action in the hunt in which a sharing of the proceeds occurs may well be balanced with familial productivity in agriculture and perhaps herding, though even here the weight of the evidence seems to be towards communal ownership. If each family had an adult male member in the hunt and an adult female in the fields as its contribution to subsistence seeking, there would be a balance of family to family—each being equal over the long run in energy output and material return. But what about families where adults have died? Those families are then out of balance with the others. In a band society or a tribe, communal sharing is part of the moral order. Thus the advantaged and the disadvantaged are equalized.

Çatal Hüyük is the site of a tightly nucleated society made up perhaps of 600 households. It can be assumed that these households had consanguinal relationships across the community, divided perhaps according to sodalities. Extended families (including the families of brothers or sisters) may well have been the basic economic unit. With the presence of sodalities, however, even if the nuclear family lost one of its adult members, the sodality to which the deceased belonged incurred an obligation to aid that family. Thus the sodality and the extended family were the assurance of familial survival. The male sodalities apparently shared the hunt; it is not clear whether they also shared the harvest. Neither is it clear—if obsidian was the basis of commerce—who obtained the raw material: individual families, special groups, or the whole community. It is these economic problems and their apparent solution in the obvious uniformity of goods used from house to house in the site that makes possible the postulation of reciprocity as a fundamental part of the economic structure. But if sodalities and special groups or traders are considered as important to the economic picture, it is also necessary to consider the problems of regulation. To make viable the distribution of goods and services in a tightly nucleated population of 3,000, an organizing head would have to be involved—not so much to regulate exchange as to keep it organized when its natural and free operation was impeded by events. Here, then, the chief stands forth providing the leadership necessary. The difference in funerary furniture seems to confirm that social status on the basis of importance to the society was an individual matter and not that of a class. The redistributional system appears to have been used to confirm egalitarianism and reinforce community. Paradoxically, the system seems to have been

supervised by a chief whose role was determined by a tribal morality which gave him prestige but little power after the needs for
which his leadership was required had been met.

In Çatal Hüyük pure reciprocity seems to have been giving
way to a redistributive system in which the values of reciprocity
were nevertheless retained, thus preserving the communal character of the society. That character was made cohesive by a moral
order in its social relations and by egalitarianism in its economic
relations.

8

The Meaning
of Çatal Hüyük

IN RETROSPECT THE WORLD of Çatal Hüyük is obviously a world
apart from those of Terra Amata and Dolni Vestonice. Yet Çatal
Hüyük contains much that is familiar in the former sites: the sense
of immediacy in man-environment relations, the dependence on a
relatively simple technology, the strong egalitarian thrust in human
relations, the moral cohesiveness, the consummate understanding
of the habits of the game, the animism which underlay the various
aspects of the world view. The differences are largely related to
the degree of permanency which each obtained: for Terra Amata,
movement all through the year according to season with related
short stays in camp after camp; for Dolni Vestonice, a long winter
stay in one convenient place followed by summer wanderings; for
Çatal Hüyük, permanent settlement.

It is the fact of permanent settlement that emphasizes the
unique position of Çatal Hüyük relative to the other sites. Permanency sets forth a special series of demands specifically different
from those required by nonpermanence: a secured local subsistence, a perennial adaptation to the change of seasons, dependable

protection from possible depredations of man and beast, endurance against the physical perils that human clustering creates (such as disease), social forms which make the community cohesive in spite of personality conflict and the differentials which varied talents, intelligence, and ages create, ideological uniformity in the face of heterogeneous ideas imposed by outside influences, effective leadership in all the varied activities, essential and otherwise, which the community participates in. When people live together in the same place, property becomes important; although at Çatal Hüyük there is no evidence for classes based on wealth, it is evident that family-owned houses were characteristic of the community. It is not likely that this was reflected in family-owned agricultural land, herds, and other material possessions; the egalitarian quality of the settlement suggests otherwise. It evidences a communal life based on common purpose, leadership, and belief with a high degree of familial privacy. The family in fact seems to have been what the anthropologist calls ambilateral; that is, what property there was could be inherited through either the father or the mother. Furthermore it would appear that at least some married children would reside with the parents to insure the continuance of familial residence in the ancestral home in which the very ancestors were buried. It is the evidence for durability of residence that suggests that a powerful force for a communal society was the kinship system. In view of the high death rate it must have been that families were from time to time deprived of consanguine descendants as sons and daughters died off. In some societies this familial crisis is met by the adoption of sons and daughters from other families, who then are given their new family's name and are fully recognized as children of their adopted family by society. Furthermore, the need for offspring to insure continuance must have made marriage among the families a significant cohesive element in the community. One can imagine all kinds of elaborate arrangements made to insure early and proper marriage which could extend kin ties across the whole community. Clearly one's individual identity rested in part on one's successful role as a procreator—a factor for prestige and security.

It is the evidence for sodalities that emphasizes a special adaptive response to the demands put forth by permanency, whether or not such sodalities had their genesis in that permanency. Hitherto the nuclear family and its expansion into that larger familial entity, the band, has seemingly characterized the prehistoric social systems. At Çatal Hüyük there are nonfamilial social entities to which the individual owed his allegiances as well as to his immediate family. Present knowledge of primitive social organization evidences that very often these entities, the sodalities, give the ultimate identity to the individual by their acknowledgment of his membership in them. The sodality, familial as it might appear to be with its stated kin relationships, its "brotherhood" or "sisterhood," has the effect of placing the individual in a larger-than-family sphere of activity, in which the individual's aspirations and accomplishments (and failures) are given communal recognition. The individual's motivations, no longer simply familial, now have community meaning.

Çatal Hüyük, then, is evidence for the holistic growth of culture. The technology, the economic system, the social organization, the religious beliefs, the leadership are all at a high level of complexity. Each of these cultural sectors is in touch with the other. But both separately and as a whole the cultural parts evidence something but barely suggested at Dolni Vestonice: a struggle for individual identity. An individual would have had identity as a child procreated by an already identified mother and father, as a young person fulfilling a role as a member of the work group, as a person who marries and procreates, and as a member of a society above and beyond his family which required the fulfillment of special obligations. Such obligations would have been not merely man-sanctioned but related to the supernatural, so that the individual would have a powerful sense that everything he did could have immortal consequence. Whatever the exact situation may have been, it is clear that the individual was rewarded with status and probably privilege in the achievement of his duties and thus in the final account had a substantive personal identity in society.

But there is another identity suggested by the evidence from Çatal Hüyük. It is that achieved when an individual has provided the family with descendants to continue the family. The succession of houses, the relative conservativism of artifacts, the durable continuing habitation of the site, and the familial graves within the houses evidence a sense of passing time in which one's existence is but temporary. This idea is certainly supported by the solid evidence for a high death rate and the perhaps less secure evidence for a concept of life in death and death in life. A society that frequently witnessed early death and yet brought the dead into the home as a means of insuring a specific relationship to the living must have been time-conscious. Time in this sense is not an abstract; it is something measured by man's life in space. Life and space have reality, and time does not exist without them. Time is also cumulative: what has come before is the foundation for what is now—but the *now* contains an obligation to make a tomorrow possible. The individual has an identity as a link in the life and space causality. The evidence at Çatal Hüyük more than suggests that individual identity in time, perhaps given particular quality by great deeds or special community recognition, was a part of the cultural consciousness.

Time consciousness adds another dimension to a culture's world view. At one time man's view of self was apparently geared to the pragmatic "now," or "a few moons ago," or "his father's son." In this sense self in space can be likened to a plate having three dimensions, the last, i.e., height, being a mere fingertip's span. With time consciousness, the plate becomes a bowl as the vertical dimension grows. Man aware of history transcends his own time and gains another means of social identity.

An important stage in the development of cognition in prehistory is marked by the ikonic culture at Çatal Hüyük. Man found self, it seems, by an image-making and perceiving process. As a member of a family, of a group, of a large society, his identity was one of being, of service, of obligations fulfilled; as an individual he was a conscious link in the cycle of life with the past and the future; as a citizen in a permanent physical situation at the center of a heterogeneous world, he was a member of an in-group which set him apart; as an individual it is clear he was aware of vulnerability to supernatural forces, forces which recognized his identity as a person possessing attributes of good or bad meaning to society.

The world of prehistoric Çatal Hüyük was still predominantly an enactive world. But it was also a world that admitted a degree of symbolism, not only in its graphic art but in the very character of the settlement itself. There were many abstractions relating to human values and ideas. The language of the time had to encompass the complexities of economic life, the meaning of life and death as then understood, the social relationships which made communal life possible, the directional vocabulary inherent in varied leadership, and the different terms and emphases necessary to communication amid the family and the sodality. But what is obvious for language is not so in other spheres of human relationships. It will be a task for the future to find the level of symbolism which existed at Çatal Hüyük. Whatever that level was, and it was not low, it was nonetheless subordinate to the immediacy of image perception that characterized life there.

9

At the Threshold
of Civilization

THE COMPARISON OF SITES remote in time and space from one
another is a comparison based on the randomness of archaeological
discovery. How near this randomness is to the actual sequential
development of man's cultures may be known when more evidence is unearthed. It is already clear that the advances of one time
become the basis of the next. Terra Amata, Dolni Vestonice, and
Çatal Hüyük stand in sequential relationship, for each represents
an advance in man's progress which is clearly incorporated in what
temporally follows.

All the evidence points to the indisputable fact that in the
sequential development of culture there was an accompanying
growth of human cognition. This growth was not linear, as in the
history of technology, but multidimensional, in keeping with the
character of the human mind and the nuances of human behavior.
For every innovation made in response to living in a physical environment, in a society, or in a culture, the human mind was forced
to consider past, present, and future in ways different from before.
Time forces itself on man whatever the character of his culture.

Time is the ultimate abstraction, yet its presence is everywhere to behold. Man's response to time has been to evolve by changing his way of life according to ever newer understandings of his place in the universe. Among the case studies examined in this book, the people of Çatal Hüyük stand forth as masters of new complexities in a stress-filled world, such masters that for almost a thousand years cultural stability was maintained and an unknown degree of happiness was achieved, as the exuberant murals suggest. In that thousand years they and their counterparts elsewhere in Afro-Eurasia built up a body of experience relating to the whole of life out of which another advance could be made. This advance would include such developments as settlements with large populations, structured social organizations, more complex technology, institutionalized leadership, the expansion of sedentarism, the growth of sophistication in ideology, and the quantitative accumulation of symbolic responses. It was not out of Çatal Hüyük that these developments sprang, but it was *because* of Çatal Hüyük and its contemporaries that the developments could occur. Their occurrence moved men farther along on the road to civilization.

In terms of the development of cultural cognition and its effect upon the individual, Terra Amata is clearly an enactive culture, remote from Dolni Vestonice and Çatal Hüyük not just temporally but in all aspects of cultural function. This remoteness cannot, however, be said to exist between Dolni Vestonice and Çatal Hüyük, particularly in the area of food production. Dolni Vestonice's people possessed the technological means to process the cereals (grinding stones, sickles, containers, fire). They even made baked clay objects. They also had the social organization. If they had selected out only young male mammoths for slaughter in order to control the population of the mammoth herd, mammalogists would be hard put not to label this selective device a domesticating mechanism. As it is, the concentration on a given animal has a domestication potential. There is a similarity between the Gravettian Venus of Dolni Vestonice and the "goddesses" of Çatal Hüyük and perhaps thereby a similar concept of fertility.

It can be argued that the Gravettians were not present in the critical nuclear areas which were the settings for primary food production. Yet one can argue that even had the culture represented by Dolni Vestonice been situated in the hilly flank zones it is unlikely that they would have pioneered food production. Their stage of incipience was not at a level of cultural awareness by which a transformation would have become necessary. There were no anomalies in their world understanding whose resolution might well have moved them to take the step to village farming over fifteen thousand years before it was taken. The people of Dolni Vestonice are representative of an early phase of ikonic culture sufficiently removed from abstract demands so that their few symbols were sufficient.

The people of Çatal Hüyük stood in the midst of an ikonic awareness of nature and themselves. But there were anomalies, caused in part by large population, the need for increased food production, the incursion of disease, and the development of community. More important, it appears that there was a world awareness more universal in meaning than that of Dolni Vestonice and that this awareness was a symptom of a new incipience, one for civilization.

But the trail through the prehistoric wilderness does not so far end in civilization. Its course only suggests that what has happened is prologue to that achievement. The next turn along the trail may open the way—and may indicate which of the two visions—materialistic and godless, or humane and god-filled—is man's true vision.

Social scientists may take exception to parts of my interpretation of prehistoric evidence; nevertheless, all must agree that there is clear evidence for growing complexity in all areas of human life and with this complexity a developing awareness of man's place in space and in time: Religious belief develops along with technology, social relationships evolve far beyond the enactive, as does man's economic activity. There is direction, then, both to greater cultural complexity and to keener perception of individual place in ever larger societies and in an expanding material world. For whereas enactivity is material, physical activity, often not far from innate behavior in its physiological motivations, ikonic behavior is a full step away from the physical. Though it has a powerful current of individual self-recognition, it also conceives of a society of individuals whose personalities are to be recognized in varied ways. It senses the human spirit much as it recognizes the energies of all the objects of the world about, those vital parts which give them their identity. Ikonic perception gives all things their place. It is thus of moment that the first truly ikonic culture which prehistorians can fully describe evidences a knowledge of time and man in relation to it. Man gives himself a place not only in space but also in a tradition. In this multidimensional context time, space, and man are not abstract symbols but full-blown realities.

Yet it is not as realities that symbolic culture—the next stage— views these entities, but as abstractions. In the transition from the cultural level represented at Çatal Hüyük to that of the present time, there had to be a struggle to keep man in focus as a reality and not an abstraction. This struggle was a social and intellectual one but, more important, was a struggle within the individual striving for self-identity. Here, then, is another direction in human history, the reduction of man to an abstraction from a living, feeling entity with easy identity at many levels. Modern man has lost perception of self in that struggle, for he can no longer be identified in the complexity wrought by symbolic cultures.

Paradoxically, however, the very abstraction which destroys identity eventually makes identity possible, for in the refusal to be lost in a new wilderness after millennia of struggle to emerge from that of prehistory, feeling man finds a new identity. It is one that makes possible the perception of time and space in a new and unique way. From those far days of primate enactivism the tortuous course has led man through the emergence of human enactivism, the dawn of self-perception, civilization's struggle for identity, to the labyrinth of abstract symbolism and the loss of self.

Now it leads into other dimensions, where the human brain perceives man as either machine or an aspect of the divine. There is no doubt that this history of man has been cumulative; each stage of knowledge and self-awareness is more amply endowed than that which preceded it. The fact that cultural evolution apparently selects for such developing understanding gives promise that a new man will emerge more aware of the meaning of man's place in time and space than any before him. It is to him one must turn one day to find the answer as to the real vision of man's destiny. The fact that all that has gone on before the dawn of civilization is witness to the evolution of all parts of certain precivilized lineages powerfully suggests that it is the humane, god-filled vision of man that is the true vision. For all civilized men of conscience are not content with the absence of the divine and the worship of the material. Their existence in our midst is the result not of biological caprice but of the steady growth of the realization that man, organic as his existence is, is not dependent on his technology or any other materialism for the knowledge which provokes his thoughts but rather upon the totality of the human experience—which totality is mirrored in the culture of which he is a part. That culture, whatever its character, proclaims man as conceiver, energizer, and historian, and not mere engineer. Prehistory evidences that civilization, whatever its immediate genesis, was the result of the complexity of the life of *Homo sapiens* who, not able to live as other primates by bread alone, took a unique evolutionary path and as if driven by forces beyond his ken rose from mere knowledge of a physical universe based on proximity to conceptions of a world of the mind, untouched by the vagaries of the primate senses for which paradoxically they owe their ultimate origin.

Appendix: Tables

Reference Notes

Bibliography

Index

Appendix: Tables

Table 1
Cognitive Stages in Selected Cultural Sectors and Categories

	Cognitive Stage		
	Enactive	**Ikonic**	**Symbolic**
Setting			
Geographic emphasis	seacoasts, rivers, lakes	inland areas, alluvial, steppe lands	universal
Residential territory	landscape	adjacent to exploitable lands	urban environment
Territory size	small	large	very large
Group size	10–100 people (median 40)	150–6,000 people (median 300)	6,500–100,000 + people
Birthrate	high	high	lower
Death rate	high	lower	much lower

215

Table 1 (Continued)
Cognitive Stages in Selected Cultural Sectors and Categories

	Cognitive Stage		
	Enactive	**Ikonic**	**Symbolic**
Setting (Continued)			
Shelter	temporary multiple family residence units	permanent units for multiple families	temporary and permanent multiple units for individual residence
Population density	less than 3 per square mile	3–16 per square mile	more than 18 per square mile
Geographic zones	tropical	temperate	universal
Life expentancy	less than 25 years	less than 35 years	less than 45 years
Public buildings	none	few	many
The Individual			
Role setting	familial	societal	institutional
Learning mechanism	imitation	precept	education
Oral language	gesture with some vocalization	vocalization with gesture	vocalization
Vocabulary reference	environmental	social	universal
Vocabulary size	limited	large	very large
Written language	pictures	semasiography	phonography
Relationship of individual to environment	direct	one or two stages removed	several stages removed

Table 1 *(Continued)*
Cognitive Stages in Selected Cultural Sectors and Categories

	Cognitive Stage		
	Enactive	**Ikonic**	**Symbolic**
Community			
Social organization	band	tribe and village	city and state
Social communication	tactile	auditory	ocular
Basis of social relationships	moral obligation	moral concept	law and ethics
Social contract	family	society	institution
Sex role	patrilocal, egalitarian	patrilocal with male dominance	bilateral
Social inattention	little	some	much
Social stratification basis	none	kin and property	occupation, wealth
Reinforcement of social status	success	prestige	power
Inheritance	familial	patrilineal	bilateral
Authority			
Polity character	egalitarianism, temporary leaders	chieftainship, headman	monarchy, republicanism, fascism
Sources of power	personal qualities	property and kin	institutional status
Political power	equally distributed	based on property, kin, and force	based on class, wealth, and force

Table 1 (Continued)
Cognitive Stages in Selected Cultural Sectors and Categories

	Cognitive Stage		
	Enactive	Ikonic	Symbolic
Authority (Continued)			
Degree of aggression	little	some	much
Form of aggression	feuding	raiding	warfare
Concentration of energy	collective, cooperative	collective, coercive	collective, institutional
Ideology			
Basis of religion	animism	pantheism	monotheism, agnosticism
Rites of passage	nonceremonial	religious rites and ceremonies	nonreligious ritualization
Rational thought	empirical	religious rationality	scientific rationality
Phenomenology	mana and animism	natural law, divine law	natural law, material absolutes
Concept of time	globular	cyclic-linear	linear-historical
Time most valued	present	past-present (tradition)	present-future
Number	notation (sets)	arithmetic	mathematics
Applied medicine	placebo effect	pharmacopoeia material	physiological and chemical treatment
Medical practitioner	shaman	priest	physician (scientist)
Communication of world view	narrative mythology	mythology, legend	literature

	Cognitive Stage		
	Enactive	**Ikonic**	**Symbolic**
Ideology (Continued)			
Communicant of world view	the individual empirically	the storyteller and the priest	the author
Orientation of world view	spirit centered	man centered	material centered, impersonal
Economics			
Economic organization	hunting and gathering	herding and farming	commerce and industry
Economic systems	reciprocal	redistributive	market (open and regulated)
Division of labor	sex and age groups	limited specialization	great specialization
Structure of productive units	family household	clan, group	political and economic organizations
Membership productive units	household members	kin, group members, "strangers"	managers and laborers
Type of wealth and capital	manpower	land and livestock	means of production, money
Control of wealth and capital	family	kin, inheritance, marriage	contract, sale conveyance, etd.
Media of exchange	gifts in kind	goods and services	monetization
Portion of population free of subsistence activity	0–2%	10–60%	98%
Frequency of craft (industrial) specialization (average)	2%	33%	100%

Table 1 *(Continued)*
Cognitive Stages in Selected Cultural Sectors and Categories

	Cognitive Stage		
	Enactive	**Ikonic**	**Symbolic**
Technology			
Tools	primary	secondary	standardization (multiple steps)
Specialization	none to few	limited	great
Energy sources	man	animals, water, wind, fire	fossil fuels
Metal use	0–10%	11–80%	100%
Metal processes	hammering	smelting and casting	alloying
Transportation types	walking and man-motivated methods	animal and wind (sail)	steam engine, gasoline engine air, sea, land
Speed of transportation	3–8 mph	6–18 mph	20+ mph
Arts			
Graphic development	primitive	archaic	classic
Graphic forms	representational	iconographic	"aesthetic" schools
Music development	rhythm	melody	harmony
Musical instruments	percussion and wind	stringed	organs, pianos, and other chording instruments
Musical practitioners	spontaneous individual	special group	professional
Music participation	individual	group	virtuoso-audience

Table 1 *(Concluded)*
Cognitive Stages in Selected Cultural Sectors and Categories

	Cognitive State		
	Enactive	**Ikonic**	**Symbolic**
Arts (Continued)			
Costume purpose	insulation, modesty	status	conformity, style
Games	physical, competitive games	games of chance	games of strategy
Drama as:	story	ritual	life
Distribution of Cultural Traits			
Positive	90%	80%	65%
Negative	10%	15%	25%
Irrelevant	—	5%	10%
Cultural change rate	slight	slow	rapid

Table 2
Relative Chronology in Prehistory

Years Before Present	Cultural Level	Hominid Forms	Western Asia Climate	Western Asia Technology	Sites
5,200	First civilizations		Essentially modern; wetter phases early in period	farming and herding	Egypt and Sumeria
7,000					Çatal Hüyük, Jarmo
10,000	beginning of food production				Natufian sites
14,000	end of Pleistocene		Würm glacial stage	Upper Paleolithic industries	Dolni Vestonice
	cave paintings			Mousterian industries	
100,000		*Homo sapiens sapiens*			
			Riss glacial stage	Acheulean core tools	
250,000		*Homo sapiens*			Olduwai IV
		latest *Homo erectus*	Mindel glacial stage	Abbevillian core tools	Terra Amata
500,000			Günz glacial stage		
1 million					
1.5 million		*Homo erectus*		flake tools	Olduwai I (?)
		latest *Australopithecus*	Donau	pebble tools	
3 million	Plio-Pleistocene boundary				
5 million	Pliocene	*Australopithecus*			
14 million	Miocene	*Ramapithecus* (earliest hominid)			

Table 3
Some Possible Interpretations of Paleolithic "Venuses"

Area	Motivation	Use	Time	Concept
Economic	continuity of human life	invocation as special deity — tutelary	according to need	human fertility*
Ideological	continuity of all life	diety (universal)	seasonal	universal fertility†
Sexual	sexual stimulation	sympathetic magic	according to need	relation of sex to fertility
Technological	to bring luck in hunting by contact with weapons	sympathetic magic	according to need	fertility as a good
Mythical	myth reinforcement	evocative	annual rate	explanation of the cosmos
Political	reinforcement of leader's authority	symbolic use (as staff or baton)	reinforcement occasions	fertility as a good
Social organization	reinforcement of kin relationships	totemic emblem	seasonal gathering of group	sense of past, present, and

* Details may differ from place to place, but form is essentially the same.
† Form is completely abstract — no face, leg, or arm differentiation.

223

Table 4
Use of Materials at Çatal Hüyük

Material	Object Obtained	Process Used
Clay	brick	molding and baking
	pottery	oven-firing, coiling, and burnishing
	maceheads	oven-firing
	slingstones, balls, beads, figurines	molding and baking
	pendants and amulets, stamp seals, statuettes	carving, molding, and baking
Stone obsidian	scrapers, chisels, burins, sickle blades, knives, daggers, arrowheads, gouges	percussion and pressure flaking
	mirrors, statuettes, maceheads	grinding and polishing
	beads	drilling
flint	daggers, scrapers, knives, firestones	percussion and pressure flaking
greenstone	axes, adzes, chisels, hoes	grinding and polishing
volcanic rocks, calcite, alabaster, marble, limestone, sandstone	saddle querns, rubbing stones, mortars and pestles polishing stones, stone rings, bracelets, plaster, maceheads	grinding, polishing, and perforating (drilling)
Ore minerals copper	beads, pendants, rings, tubes blue-green pigment, sheeting	grinding, polishing, smelting(?), and hammering
iron	red, yellow, and red-brown pigments	grinding and mixing

Table 4 *(Continued)*
Use of Materials at Çatal Hüyük

Material	Object Obtained	Process Used
Ore minerals (cont.) lead	beads, pendants, tubes	roasting
	gray pigments	grinding
manganese	purple pigment	grinding
mercury	red pigment	grinding
lignite	fuel (?)	burning
soot	black pigment	grinding
apatite	beads	grinding and drilling
carnelian	beads	grinding and drilling
rock crystal	?	grinding and drilling
sulfur	(for fire making)	grinding and drilling
Reeds, rushes, straw, grass	string, thread, rope, felt	spinning, twining
	mats and carpets	weaving (quadruple warp and weft), combing
	textiles, nets (?)	weaving, sewing, knotting
	basketry	spiraling, coiling, sewing
	fuel	burning
Bone	cups, hafts, scoops, pendants and amulets, ladles, spatulas, cosmetic tools, pins, needles, awls, punches, polishes, wristguards, hooks and eyes, ointment sticks, beads, rings	polishing, carving, incising, punching, drilling
Antler	toggles, sickle hafts	carving
Tusk (boar)	collars, bracelets	carving

Table 4 *(Continued)*
Use of Materials at Çatal Hüyük

Material	Object Obtained	Process Uses
Leather	footwear (?), belts, sheaths, slings, bowstrings	cutting and scraping, punching, tanning (acorns), drying, curing
	nets	knotting
Fur and skin (leopard)	capes (?), skirts, emblems, caps	scraping, drying, tanning (?)
Hair, wool	textiles, rugs, and hangins	weaving, knotting, twining, sewing, stamping, combing
Shell (dentalium, cardium, cowrie, whelk)	beads	drilling, grinding, polishing
Wood oak, juniper	timber	sawing, chopping, adzing carving
fir	vessels, boxes, pins	sawing, chopping, adzing, carving
Fruit almonds	oil	grinding, pressing
acorns	tannin	grinding, pressing
pistachio *(Pistacia atlantica),* apple, juniper	food	
juniper	aromate	
hackberry	wine	fermenting

Table 4 (Continued)
Use of Materials at Çatal Hüyük

Material	Object Obtained	Process Used
Food plants emmer	flour	planting, threshing, storing, sieving, grinding
	beer	fermenting
einkorn, six-rowed barley, bread wheat *(Triticum sestivum)*	flour	planting, threshing, storing, sieving, grinding
field pea *(Pisum elatius)*, lentils, vetch *(Vicia noena)*, bitter vetch *(Ervum ervilia)*	flour (peas and pod)	shelling, grinding (uncultivated)
shepherd's purse *(Capsella bursa-pastoris)*, ervsimum, sisymbriodes	fat	
Other plants madder *(Rubia tinctorum)*	red dye	grinding
woad *(isatis tinctorum)*	blue dye	grinding and fermenting
weld *(Reseda luteola)*	yellow dye	grinding
flax (?)	textile, linseed	
Domesticated animals dog	protection	training
goat	food, milk (?), hair, skin	milking, shearing, skimming

Table 4 *(Concluded)*
Use of Materials at Catal Hüyük

Material	Object Obtained	Process Used
Domesticated animals (cont.) sheep	food, hair	shearing
cattle	food, bone	
Wild animals aurochs (*Bos primigenius),* pig *(Sus scrofa),* red deer *(Cervus elaphus),* wild ass (two species), roe deer, fallow deer, ibex, gazelle	food, skin, bone, tusk, fat	hunting and trapping
fox, wolf	(ritual)	
leopard	skin	
bear (?)		
weasel		
fish		
bees	honey, wax	fermenting (?)
mouse, shrew	(pest)	
snake		
Birds black crane, vulture	(ritual)	
	eggs (?)	

Table 5
Manufacture and Usage of Objects Found at Çatal Hüyük

Objects	Use	User	Maker
adzes	cutting	carpenter	stoneworker
amulets	protection	society — mostly females	religious practitioner
arrows and arrowheads	hunting and protection	hunters and warriors	stoneworker
awls	holemaking in various materials	society	general
axes	cutting	carpenter or tree-feller	stoneworker
balls, clay	toys (?)	children	general
balls, stone	digging	farmer	stoneworker
baskets	container	household	basketmaker, female
beads: clay, bone, stone, metal	adornment or status indicator	household female (generally)	general; metal ones by specialists
beer	beverage	household	general
belts	waistband	household	weaver; leather-worker
bows	hunting and protection	hunters and warriors	bowmakers
bowstrings	hunting and protection	hunters and warriors	bowmakers
boxes, wooden	container	household	carpenter
braclets: bone, stone, metal	adornment or status indicator	household	general; metal ones by specialists
burins	cutting (wood or skins)	carpenter and	general

Table 5 *(Continued)*
Manufacture and Usage of Objects Found at Çatal Hüyük

Objects	Use	User	Maker
caps or hats	status indicator	hunter and specialist	skin and fur specialist
carpets	floor and wall covering	household and shrine	weaver
chisels	cutting	carpenter	stoneworker
collars	status indicator	specialist	religious practitioner
combs	weaving and personal use	weaver and household	carpenter
cosmetics	adornment and status indicator	household and specialist	general female
cups: wooden, pottery	containers,	household	carpenter, potter
daggers	hunting and protection	hunters and warriors	stoneworker
drums	hunting and dance	hunters and warriors	specialist
dyes	coloring (body and textiles)	household	general, weaver
figurines, clay	toys and religious objects	children and household	general and religious practitioner
firestones	firemaking	household	general
footwear	clothing	household	leatherworker
gouges	cutting	carpenter	stoneworker
hearth	cooking and heat, light	household	general
hoes	farming	household (female)	stoneworker

Objects	Use	User	Maker
hooks and eyes	clothing and equipment	household (male)	general
knives, stone	general	household	general and stoneworker
ladies (spoons), wooden	spooning	household female	carpenter
maceheads	hunting and protection	hunters and warriors	stoneworker
mats	general covering	household	weavers and general
mirrors	adornment and religious use	religious practitioner, female	special stoneworker
mortars and pestles	pounding	household and craftsmen	general
needles	sewing	household	general
nets	hunting	hunters	weaver
ointment	adornment and healing	household	general
ointment sticks (cosmetic tools)	adornment and healing	household	general; metal ones by specialists
ovens: wall and courtyard	cooking and baking	household	general
pendants: clay stone, bone	protection and adornment	household	general and religious practitioner
pigments: mural, body, and pottery	painting	specialist, household, potter	painter, specialist, general
pins	clothing	household	general, female

Table 5 *(Continued)*
Manufacture and Usage of Objects Found at Çatal Hüyük

Objects	Use	User	Maker
plaster	wall and floor covering	household shrines	general and specialist modeler
polishing stones	many activities	household and special crafts	general
pottery	containers	household	potter
punches and drills	many activities	household	general
querns, saddle	cereal grinding	household	general
rings, stone	agriculture	household, female	stoneworker
rings, copper	adornment	household, female	metalworker
rope	general	household	weaver
rubbing stones	polishing and grinding	household	general
saws, stone	cutting	carpenter	stoneworker
scoops, wood	household	household	carpenter
scrapers, stone	general	household	general
seals, stamp	textile-making; status indicators	wearer, specialist	sealmaker
skins: leopard and other	status indicator clothing	hunter, general	hunter and leatherworker
sheeting, copper	rings, etc.	general	metalworker
sheaths	general	hunter and warrior	leatherworker
sickles	cutting	farmer and gatherer	general
slings and slingstones	hunting and warfare	hunter and warrior	general

Table 5 (Concluded)
Manufacture and Usage of Objects Found at Çatal Hüyük

Objects	Use	User	Maker
spatulas	cooking and weaving	household (female)	general
spears	hunting and warfare	hunter and warrior	stoneworker (best examples); general
statuettes: stone and clay	religious use	religious practitioner	cult specialist
sting	general	household	weaver
textiles: animal and plant	general	household	weaver
thread	general	household	weaver
toggles	clothing	men	general
tubes	adornment	household	metalworker
vessels: wool and stone	containers	household	carpenter, stoneworker
wine	general	household	general
wristguards	hunting and warfare	hunters and warriors	general
footstuffs (cereals, peas, beans, fruit, honey, meat)	food	household	
objects related to herding	herding	children	general
objects related to hunting	hunting	men	general
objects related to planting	planting	women	general

Reference Notes

INTRODUCTION

1. Winston S. Churchill, *A History of the English-Speaking Peoples,* vol. 1 (New York: Dodd, Mead, 1956), pp. 6–7.
2. See, for example, Robert J. Braidwood, *Prehistoric Men,* 7th ed. (Glenview, Ill.: Scott, Foresman, 1967), pp. 136–137.
3. Sigmund Freud, *Civilization and Its Discontents,* ed. and trans. James Strachey (New York: Norton, 1961), pp. 44–46.
4. See, for example, Lewis Mumford, *The Transformations of Man,* World Perspectives Series, vol. 7 (New York: Harper, 1936), pp. 44–46.
5. Robert Redfield, *The Primitive World and Its Transformations* (Ithaca: Cornell University Press, 1953), p. 23.
6. See, for example, A. J. Toynbee, *A Study of History* (New York: Oxford University Press, 1957).
7. Alfred N. Whitehead, *Adventures of Ideas* (New York: Macmillan, 1933), pp. 364–365.
8. Ralph Waldo Emerson, *Society and Solitude* (Boston: Houghton, Mifflin, 1870); Rudyard Kipling, *A Book of Words* (New York: Doubleday, 1925), pp. 191–192; George P. Landow, *The Aesthetic and Critical Theories of John Ruskin* (Princeton: Princeton University Press, 1971); T. S. Eliot, *Notes towards the Definition of Culture* (New York: Harcourt, 1949); Clive Bell, *Civilization and Old Friends* (Chicago: University of Chicago Press, 1973); Bernard Berenson, *Aesthetics and History* (New York: Doubleday Anchor Books, 1948); Herbert Read, ed., *The Meaning of Art* (New York: Praeger, 1972); Kenneth Clark, *Civilisation* (New York: Harper, 1969).
9. R. G. Collingwood, *The New Leviathan* (New York: Apollo Editions, 1971).
10. See, for example, George P. Adams, "The Idea of Civilization," in *Civiliza-*

tion, ed. V. F. Lenzen et al. (Berkeley: University of California Press, 1959), pp. 52–53.
11. Pierre Teilhard de Chardin, *The Phenomenon of Man* (New York: Harper Torch Books, 1959).
12. James B. Conant, ed., *Harvard Case Studies in Experimental Science* (Cambridge, Mass.: Harvard University Press, 1966); Thomas S. Kuhn, "The Structure of Scientific Revolutions," in *International Encyclopedia of Unified Science,* 2d ed., vol. 2., no. 2 (Chicago: University of Chicago Press, 1970); Arnold Brecht, *Political Theory* (Princeton: Princeton University Press, 1967).

CHAPTER 1. The Two Visions of Man

1. Jerome S. Bruner, *Studies in Cognitive Growth* (New York: Wiley, 1966).
2. Jacob Bronowski, "New Concepts in the Evolution of Complexity: Stratified Stability and Unbounded Plans," *Zygon* 5, no. 1 (March 1970), p. 34.

CHAPTER 2. The Dawn of Cognition

1. George P. Murdock, "The Common Denominator of Cultures," in *Perspectives on Human Evolution,* ed. S. C. Washburn and P. C. Jay (New York: Holt, Rinehart & Winston, 1968), p. 231.

CHAPTER 3. The Stages of Cognition

1. I. J. Gelb, *A Study of Writing,* rev. ed. (Chicago: University of Chicago Press, 1963), p. 11.

CHAPTER 4. Terra Amata

1. Henry de Lumley, "Les Fouilles de Terra Amata à Nice," *Bulletin du Musée d'Anthropologie préhistorique de Monaco* 13 (1966):29–51, and "A Paleolithic Camp at Nice," *Scientific American,* May 1969, p. 42.
2. Carl O. Sauer, "Seashore—Primitive Home of Man?," *Proceedings of the American Philosophical Society* 106, no. 1 (1962), pp. 41–47; see also Euell Gibbons, *Stalking the Blue-Eyed Scallop* (New York: McKay, 1964).
3. George Schaller and Gordon R. Lowther, "The Relevance of Carnivore Behavior to the Study of Early Hominids," *Southwestern Journal of Anthropology* 25, no. 4 (1969), pp. 307–341.
4. Brent Berlin and Paul Kay, *Basic Color Terms* (Berkeley: University of California Press, 1969).

CHAPTER 5. Dolni Vestonice

1. Bohuslav Klima, *Dolni Vestonice: Exploration of a Camp of Mammoth Hunters in 1947–1952,* Monumenta Archaeologica, vol. 11 (Prague: Archaeological Institute of the Czechoslovak Academy of Sciences, 1963), and "The First Ground-Plan of an Upper Paleolithic Loess Settlement in Middle Europe and Its Meaning," in *Courses Toward Urban Life,* ed. R. J. Braid-

wood and G. R. Willey, Viking Fund Publications in Anthropology, vol. 32 (Chicago: Aldine, 1962), pp. 193–210.

2. Henry Fairfield Osborn, *Proboscidea* (New York: American Museum of Natural History, 1942), 2:929.

3. Irven O. Buss, "Some Observations on Food Habits and Behavior of the African Elephant," *Journal of Wildlife Management* 25 (January 1961): 131–148.

4. J. L. Cloudsley-Thompson, *The Zoology of Tropical Africa* (New York: Norton, 1969), p. 86.

5. Buss, "Food Habits and Behavior of the African Elephant," *Journal of Wildlife Management* 25 (January 1961):131–148; D. F. Vesey-Fitzgerald, "Grazing Succession among East African Game Animals," *Journal of Mammalogy* 41, no. 2 (May 1960), pp. 161–172.

6. H. K. Buechner et al., "Numbers and Migration of Elephants in Murchison Falls National Park, Uganda," *Journal of Wildlife Management* 27 (January 1963):52.

7. Buss, "Food Habits and Behavior of the African Elephant," p. 144; R. F. Ewer, *Ethology of Mammals* (New York: Plenum, 1969), p. 93.

8. Vesey-Fitzgerald, "Grazing Succession," p. 171.

9. J. G. D. Clark, *Prehistoric Europe* (New York: Philosophical Library, 1952), pp. 59–61.

10. For a summary of the caloric value of certain Pleistocene animals, see R. G. Klein, *Man and Culture in the Late Pleistocene* (San Francisco: Chandler, 1969), tables 38 and 39.

11. Karl Absolon, "Mammoth Hunters," *Illustrated London News,* 23 November 1929; see also Henry Fairfield Osborn, "On the Mammoth," *Natural History* 30, no. 3 (May–June 1930), p. 232.

12. Klima, "First Ground-Plan," p. 201.

13. J. M. Coles and E. S. Higgs, *The Archaeology of Early Man* (New York: Praeger, 1969), p. 233.

14. André Leroi-Gourhan, *Treasures of Prehistoric Art* (New York: Abrams, 1967), and "The Evolution of Paleolithic Art," *Scientific American,* February 1968, pp. 58–68, 70.

15. Alexander Marshack, *The Roots of Civilization* (New York: McGraw-Hill, 1972).

16. Asen Balikci, *The Netsilik Eskimo* (New York: Doubleday, 1971), p. 197.

17. Colin M. Turnbull, *The Forest People* (New York: Simon & Schuster, 1961), p. 93.

18. Adolphus P. Elkin, *The Australian Aborigines* (New York: Doubleday, 1964), p. 19.

19. Alfred R. Radcliffe-Brown, *The Andaman Islanders* (New York: Macmillan, 1964), p. 30.

20. Kai Donner, *Among the Samoyed in Siberia,* trans. Rinehart Kyler (New Haven: Human Relations Area Files, 1954).

21. See, for example, Charles Peabody, "Red Paint," *Journal de la Société des Américanistes de Paris* 19 (1927):207–244; and Ales Hrdlička, "A Painted Skeleton from Northern Mexico," *American Anthropologist* 3 (1901):701–725.

22. Marshack, *Roots of Civilization,* p. 302.

23. François Bordes, *The Old Stone Age* (New York: McGraw-Hill, 1968), pp. 176, 224–226.
24. See, for example, Leroi-Gourhan, *Treasures of Prehistoric Art* and "Evolution of Paleolithic Art"; Coles and Higgs, *Archaeology of Early Man*.

CHAPTER 6. Prelude to a New Life

1. J. R. Harlan, "A Wild Wheat Harvest in Turkey," *Archaeology* 20, no. 3 (1967), pp. 197–201.
2. Lewis R. Binford, "Post-Pleistocene Adaptations," in *New Perspectives in Archaeology,* ed. S. R. Binford and L. R. Binford (Chicago: Aldine, 1968), pp. 313–341.
3. Frank Hole, Kent V. Flannery, and James A. Neely, *Prehistory and Human Ecology,* Memoirs of the Museum of Anthropology, no. 1 (Ann Arbor: University of Michigan Press, 1969).
4. See in particular James Conant, ed., *Harvard Case Studies in Experimental Science* (Cambridge, Mass.: Harvard University Press, 1966); John Livingston Lowes, *The Road to Xanadu* (Boston: Houghton Mifflin, 1964).
5. Alexander Marshack, *The Roots of Civilization* (New York: McGraw-Hill, 1972).

CHAPTER 7. The Site of Çatal Hüyük

1. James Mellaart, "Çatal Hüyük—A Neolithic Town in Anatolia," in *New Aspects of Archaeology,* ed. Mortimer Wheeler (New York: McGraw-Hill, 1967).
2. A discussion of the depths reached by the cultural levels is found in Harold R. Cohen, "The Paleoecology of South Central Anatolia at the End of the Pleistocene and the Beginning of the Holocene," *Anatolian Studies* 20 (1970):123–126.
3. Mellaart, "Neolithic Town," p. 67.
4. For example, Walter C. O'Kane, *Sun in the Sky* (Norman: University of Oklahoma Press, 1950), p. 50. There are numerous other comments on pueblos in the extensive literature on the American Southwest.
5. Halet Çambel and R. J. Braidwood, "An Early Farming Village in Turkey," *Scientific American,* March 1970, pp. 50–56.
6. Alexander Marshack, "Cognitive Aspects of Upper Paleolithic Engraving," *Current Anthropology* 13 (November 1964):743–745.
7. Mellaart, "Neolithic Town," p. 77.
8. Ibid., pp. 78–79.
9. Ibid., p. 104.
10. Ibid., pp. 50–51.
11. James Mellaart, "Excavations at Çatal Hüyük: Fourth Preliminary Report," *Anatolian Studies* 16 (1966):183.
12. Mellaart, "Neolithic Town," pp. 15–26, and "A Neolithic City in Turkey," *Scientific American,* April 1964, pp. 94–104.
13. Mellaart, "Neolithic City," p. 94.
14. Mellaart, "Neolithic Town," pp. 58–60.
15. Ibid., p. 70.
16. James Mellaart, "Anatolia before 4000 B.C.," in *The Cambridge Ancient*

History, ed. I. E. S. Edwards, C. J. Gadd, and N. E. I. Hammond (Cambridge: Cambridge University Press, 1970), 1:309.

17. J. Lawrence Angel, "Early Neolithic Skeletons from Çatal Hüyük: Demography and Pathology," *Anatolian Studies* 21 (1971):77–98.
18. Discussion of questions relating to the paleoecology of the region can be found in Cohen, "Paleoecology of South Central Anatolia," pp. 119–137.
19. Suberde's site report has not yet been published. Brief accounts of the work can be found in *Anatolian Studies* 15 (1965):30–32 and 16 (1966):32–33. For the report on the animal bones see Dexter Perkins, Jr., and Patricia Daly, "A Hunter's Village in Neolithic Turkey," *Scientific American,* November 1968, p. 96.
20. Mellaart, "Fourth Preliminary Report," p. 182.
21. Mellaart, "Neolithic Town," p. 224.
22. Mellaart, "Neolithic City," p. 99.
23. Christoph Von Furer-Haimendorf, *The Konyak Nagas: An Indian Frontier Tribe* (New York: Holt, 1969), pp. 18–19.
24. See, for example, Von Furer-Haimendorf, *Konyak Nagas,* p. 19.
25. J. E. Dixon, J. R. Cann, and Colin Renfrew, "Obsidian and the Origins of Trade," *Scientific American,* March 1968, p. 43.
26. References to priesthood, for example, are found in Mellaart, "Neolithic Town," pp. 80, 175, 202, 206, 207, 211.
27. Robert L. Carneiro, "On the Relationship between Size of Population and Complexity of Social Organization," *Southwestern Journal of Anthropology* 23, no. 3 (1967), p. 239.
28. For an example of one such change, see Mellaart, "Neolithic Town," pp. 178–202.
29. Herbert Barry III, "Relations between Child Training and the Pictorial Arts," *Journal of Abnormal and Social Psychology* 54, no. 3 (May 1957), pp. 380–383; J. L. Fischer, "Art Styles as Cultural Cognitive Maps," *American Anthropology* 63, no. 1 (February 1961), pp. 79–93; Vytautaf Kavolis, "The Value-Orientations Theory of Artistic Style," *Anthropological Quarterly* 38, no. 1 (January 1965), pp. 1–19. These articles can be found in *Art and Aesthetics in Primitive Societies,* ed. Carol F. Jopling (New York: Dutton, 1971); other articles in this anthology also have bearing here.
30. Mellaart, "Fourth Preliminary Report," p. 190.
31. Mellaart, "Neolithic Town," p. 132.
32. Fischer, "Art Styles as Cultural Cognitive Maps."
33. For a discussion of qualifications and statistical validities, see Robert L. Carneiro, "Scale Analysis, Evolutionary Sequences, and the Rating of Cultures," in *A Handbook of Method in Cultural Anthropology,* ed. Raoul Haroll and Ronald Cohen (Garden City, N.Y.: Natural History Press, 1970), pp. 833–870.
34. Carneiro, "Relationship between Size and Complexity," p. 238.
35. See especially Elman R. Service, *Profiles in Ethnology* (New York: Harper and Row, 1963), and *Primitive Social Organization* (New York: Random House, 1962); Marshall D. Sahlins and E. R. Service, *Evolution and Culture* (Ann Arbor: University of Michigan Press, 1960).
36. Marshall D. Sahlins, *Tribesmen* (Englewood Cliffs, N.J.: Prentice-Hall, 1968). See also the works named in note 35.
37. Mellaart, "Fourth Preliminary Report," p. 191.

38. Sahlins, *Tribesmen*, p. 24.
39. D. H. French, "Notes on Site Distribution in the Çumra Area," *Anatolian Studies* 20 (1970):143; Ian A. Todd, "Asikli Hüyük—A Protoneolithic Site in Central Anatolia," *Anatolian Studies* 16 (1966).
40. Angel, "Early Neolithic Skeletons," pp. 77–92.
41. For discussion of the animism of primitive man, see Emile Durkheim, *The Elementary Forms of the Religious Life* (New York: Collier, 1961); Robert H. Lowie, *Primitive Religion* (New York: Grosset & Dunlap, 1952); Paul Radin, *Primitive Religion* (New York: Dover, 1957); Robert Redfield, *The Primitive World and Its Transformations* (Ithaca, N.Y.: Cornell University Press, 1953); and Henri Frankfort et al., eds., *Before Philosophy: The Intellectual Adventure of Ancient Man* (Baltimore: Penguin, 1949).
42. See especially Mellaart, "Neolithic City" and "Neolithic Town."
43. Mellaart, "Neolithic City," p. 102.
44. See, for example, A. R. Radcliffe-Brown, *The Andaman Islanders* (New York: Free Press, 1964).
45. Mellaart, "Neolithic Town," p. 204.
46. There are many important studies of sexual roles in anthropological and sociological literature. An excellent summation of some of these is D. S. Marshall and R. C. Suggs, eds., *Human Sexual Behavior* (New York: Basic Books, 1971). See in particular the article by Lee Rainwater, p. 187.
47. Two key studies in the moral order of primitive man are Redfield, *Primitive World,* and Christoph Von Furer-Haimendorf, *Morals and Merit* (Chicago: University of Chicago Press, 1967).
48. Mellaart, "Neolithic City," p. 101.
49. Manning Nash, *Primitive and Peasant Economic Systems* (Chicago: Chandler, 1966), pp. 31–33.

Bibliography

ADAMS, GEORGE P. "The Idea of Civilization." In *Civilization,* edited by V. F. Lenzen, S. C. Pepper, G. P. Adams, N. S. MacKay, E. W. Strong, A. J. Melden, and W. R. Dennes. Berkeley: University of California Press, 1959.

ADAMS, ROBERT M. *The Evolution of Urban Society.* Chicago: Aldine Atherton, 1971.

ANGEL, J. LAWRENCE. "Early Neolithic Skeletons from Çatal Hüyük: Demography and Pathology," *Anatolian Studies* 21 (1971):77–98.

ARDREY, ROBERT. *The Territorial Imperative.* New York: Atheneum, 1966.

BARRY, HERBERT. "Relationships between Child Training and the Pictorial Arts." *Journal of Abnormal and Social Psychology* 54 (1957):380–383.

BASHAM A. L. *The Wonder That Was India.* New York: Hawthorn Books, 1963.

BEALS, RALPH L., and HOIJER, HARRY. *An Introduction to Anthropology.* 4th ed. New York: Macmillan, 1971.

BERLIN, BRENT, and KAY, PAUL. *Basic Color Terms.* Berkeley: University of California Press, 1969.

BIALOR, PERRY A. "The Chipped Stone Industry of Çatal Hüyük." *Anatolian Studies* 12 (1962):67–110.

BINFORD, LEWIS R. "Post-Pleistocene Adaptations." In *New Perspectives in Archaeology,* edited by S. R. Binford and L. R. Binford. Chicago: Aldine, 1968, pp. 313–341.

BORDES, FRANÇOIS. *The Old Stone Age.* New York: World University Library, McGraw-Hill, 1968.

BOWES, ANNA DE PLANTER, and CHURCH, C. F., eds. *Food Values of Portions Commonly Used.* 9th ed. Philadelphia: Lippincott, 1963.

BRAIDWOOD, ROBERT J. "From Cave to Village, an Account of a Recent Expedition to Iraq." *Scientific American,* October 1952, pp. 62–66.

———. "The Near East and the Foundations for Civilization." London Lectures, Oregon State University, 1952.

———. "Near Eastern Prehistory." *Science* 127 (1958):1419–1430.

———. "The Agricultural Revolution." *Scientific American,* September 1960, pp. 130–148.

———. *Prehistoric Men.* 7th ed. Glenview, Illinois: Scott, Foresman, 1967.

BRAIDWOOD, ROBERT J., and BRAIDWOOD, LINDA. "Jarmo: A Village of Early Farmers in Iraq." *Antiquity* 24 (1950):189–195.

BRAIDWOOD, R. J., and HOWE, B. *Prehistoric Investigations in Iraqi Kurdistan.* The Oriental Institute, Studies in Ancient Oriental Civilizations no. 31. Chicago: University of Chicago Press, 1960.

BRAIDWOOD, R. J., and REED, CHARLES A. "The Achievement and Early Consequences of Food Production: A Consideration of the Archaeological and Natural Historical Evidence." *Cold Spring Harbor Symposia on Quantitative Biology* 22 (1957): pp. 19–31.

BRAIDWOOD, R. J., and WILLEY, G. R., eds. *Courses Toward Urban Life.* Viking Fund Publications in Anthropology, vol. 32. Chicago: Aldine, 1962.

BRUNER, J. S., *Studies in Cognitive Growth.* New York: Wiley, 1966.

BUECHNER, H. K., et al. "Numbers and Migration of Elephants in Murchison Falls National Park, Uganda." *Journal of Wildlife Management* 27 (1963):36–53.

BURNHAM, HAROLD B. "Çatal Hüyük—The Textiles and Twined Fabrics." *Anatolian Studies* 15 (1965): 169–174.

BUSS, IRVEN O. "Some Observations on Food Habits and Behavior of the African Elephant." *Journal of Wildlife Management* 25 (1961):131–148.

BUTZER, K. W. *Environment and Archaeology.* 2nd ed. Chicago: Aldine, 1971.

ÇAMBEL, HALET, and BRAIDWOOD, R. J. "An Early Farming Village in Turkey." *Scientific American,* March 1970, pp. 50–56.

CARNEIRO, ROBERT L. "On the Relationship between Size of Population and Complexity of Social Organization." *Southwestern Journal of Anthropology* 23 (1967):234–243.

———. "Scale Analysis, Evolutionary Sequences, and the Rating of Cultures." In *A Handbook of Method in Cultural Anthropology,* edited by Raoul Haroll and Ronald Cohen. Garden City, New York: Natural History Press, 1970, pp. 833–870.

CARNEIRO ROBERT L. and HILSE, DAISY F. "On Determining the Probable Rate of Population Growth during the Neolithic." *American Anthropologist* 48 (1966):177–181.

CASSIRER, ERNST. *An Essay on Man.* New Haven: Yale University Press, 1962.

CHAPPLE, ELIOT D. *Culture and Biological Man.* New York: Holt, 1970.

CHILDE, V. GORDON. *What Happened in History.* Baltimore: Penguin Books, 1942.

———. *Social Evolution.* New York: Henry Schuman, 1951.

———. *New Light on the Ancient Near East.* London: Routledge and Kegan Paul, 1952.

CHOMSKY, NOAM. Review of *Verbal Behavior,* by B. F. Skinner. In *The Structure of Language: Readings in the Philosophy of Language,* edited by J. A. Fodor and J. J. Katz. Englewood Cliffs, N. J.: Prentice-Hall, 1964.

CHURCHILL, WINSTON S. *A History of the English-Speaking Peoples,* vol. 1. New York: Dodd, Mead, 1956.

CLARK, J. G. D. *Prehistoric Europe.* New York: Philosophical Library, 1952.

CLOUDSLEY-THOMPSON, JOHN L. *The Zoology of Tropical Africa.* London: Weidenfeld & Nicolson, 1969.

COHEN, HAROLD R. "The Paleoecology of South Central Anatolia at the End of the Pleistocene and the Beginning of the Holocene." *Anatolian Studies* 20 (1970):119–137.

COLES, J. M. and HIGGS, E. S. *The Archaeology of Early Man.* New York: Praeger, 1969.

COLLINGWOOD, R. G. *The New Leviathan.* New York: Apollo Editions, 1971.

CONANT, JAMES BRYANT, ed. *Harvard Case Studies in Experimental Science.* Cambridge: Harvard University Press, 1966.

DEMEK, J., STRIDA, M., et al. *Geography of Czechoslovakia.* Prague: Czechoslovak Academy of Sciences, 1971.

DIXON, J. E., CANN, J. R., and RENFREW, COLIN. "Obsidian and the Origins of Trade," *Scientific American,* March 1968, pp. 38–46.

DOBZHANSKY, THEODOSIUS. *Mankind Evolving.* New Haven: Yale University Press, 1962.

DURKHEIM, EMILE. *The Elementary Forms of the Religious Life.* New York: Collier Books, 1961.

ELIOT, T. S. *Notes towards the Definition of Culture.* New York: Harcourt, 1949.

EWER, R. F. *Ethology of Mammals.* New York: Plenum, 1969.

FISCHER, J. L. "Art Styles as Cultural Cognitive Maps." In *Art and Aesthetics in Primitive Societies,* edited by Carol F. Jopling. New York: Dutton, 1971, pp. 171–192.

FLANNERY, KENT. "The Ecology of Early Food Production in Mesopotamia." *Science* 147 (1965):1247–1256.

————. "Origins and Ecological Effects of Early Domestication in Iran and the Near East." In *The Domestication and Exploitation of Plants and Animals,* edited by P. J. Ucko and G. W. Dimbleby. Chicago: Aldine, 1969.

FRANKFORT, H. et al. *Before Philosophy: The Intellectual Adventure of Ancient Man.* Baltimore: Penguin Books, 1949.

FRENCH, D. H. "Notes on Site Distribution in the Çumra Area." *Anatolian Studies* 20 (1970):139–148.

GELB, I. J. *A Study of Writing.* Rev. ed. Chicago: University of Chicago Press, 1963.

GIBBONS, EUELL. *Stalking the Blue-Eyed Scallop.* New York: McKay, 1964.

GRAZIOSI, PAOLO. *Paleolithic Art.* New York: McGraw-Hill, 1960.

HARLAN, J. R. "A Wild Wheat Harvest in Turkey." *Archaeology* 20, no. 3 (1967), pp. 197–201.

HARLAN, J. R., and ZOHARY, DANIEL. "Distribution of Wild Wheats and Barley." *Science* 153 (1966):1074–1080.

HARNER, M. J. "Population Pressure and the Social Evolution of Agriculturalists." *Southwestern Journal of Anthropology* 26 (1970):67–86.

HELBAEK, HANS. "Textiles from Çatal Hüyük." *Archaeology* 16 (1963):39–46.

————. "First Impressions of the Çatal Hüyük Plant Husbandry." *Anatolian Studies* 14 (1964):121–123.

HIGGS, E. S., and JARMEN, M. R. "The Origins of Agriculture: A Reconsideration." *Antiquity* 43 (1969):32–41.

HOEBEL, E. ADAMSON. *Anthropology: The Study of Man.* 4th ed. New York: McGraw-Hill, 1972.

HOLE, FRANK, and FLANNERY, KENT V. "The Prehistory of Southwestern Iran, A Preliminary Report." *Proceedings of the Prehistoric Society,* n.s. 33 (1967):147–206.

HOLE, FRANK, FLANNERY, KENT V., and NEELY, JAMES A. *Prehistory and Human Ecology of the Deh Luran Plain.* Memoirs of the Museum of Anthropology, no. 1. Ann Arbor: University of Michigan, 1969.

HOLMES, OLIVER WENDELL. "Crime and Automatism." In *Pages from an Old Volume of Life: A Collection of Essays, 1857–1881.* New ed. Boston: Houghton Mifflin, 1892.

HRDLIČKA, ALES. "A Painted Skeleton from Northern Mexico, with Notes on Bone Painting among the American Aborigines." *American Anthropologist,* n.s. 3 (1901): 701–725.

JOLLY, ALISON. *The Evolution of Primate Behavior.* New York: Macmillan, 1972.

JOPLING, CAROL F., ed. *Art and Aesthetics in Primitive Societies—A Critical Anthology.* New York: Dutton, 1971.

KAROLIS, VYTAUTAF. "The Value-Orientations Theory of Artistic Style." *Anthropological Quarterly* 38 (1965):1–19.

KENYON, KATHLEEN M. "Ancient Jericho." *Scientific American,* April 1954, pp. 76–82.

KIPLING, RUDYARD. "A Return to Civilization." In *A Book of Words: Selections from Speeches and Addresses Delivered between 1906 and 1927.* New York: Doubleday, 1928.

KIRKBRIDE, D. "Five Seasons at the Pre-Pottery Neolithic Village of Beidha, in Jordan." *Palestine Exploration Quarterly,* January–June, 1966, pp. 8–72.

KLEIN, RICHARD G. *Man and Culture in the Late Pleistocene.* San Francisco: Chandler, 1969.

KLIMA, BOHUSLAV. "The First Ground-Plan of an Upper Paleolithic Loess Settlement in Middle Europe and Its Meaning." In *Courses toward Urban Life,* edited by R. J. Braidwood and G. R. Willey. Viking Fund Publications in Anthropology, vol. 32. Chicago: Aldine, 1962, pp. 193–210.

————. *Dolni Vestonice: Exploration of a Camp of Mammoth Hunters in 1947–1952.* Monumenta Archaeologica, vol. 11. Prague: Archaeological Institute of the Czechoslovak Academy of Sciences, 1963.

KLOPFER, PETER H. *Habitats and Territories.* New York: Basic Books, 1969.

KLUCKHOHN, CLYDE. *Navaho Witchcraft.* Boston: Beacon Press, 1967.

KNOR, A., et al. *Dolni Vestonice: Vyzkum Taboriste Lovev Mamutu v Letech 1945–1947* (Dolni Vestonice: The Exploration of a Camp of Mammoth Hunters in 1945–1947). Monumenta Archaeologica, vol. 2. Prague: Archaeological Institute of the Czechoslovak Academy of Sciences, 1953.

LAWRENCE, T. E. *Seven Pillars of Wisdom.* New York: Doubleday, 1938.

LEIGHTON, DOROTHEA, and KLUCKHOHN, CLYDE. *Children of the People.* New York: Farrar, Straus, 1950.

LENSKI, GERHARD. *Human Societies—A Macrolevel Introduction to Sociology.* New York: McGraw-Hill, 1970.

LEONTIEF, WASSILY W. *Input-Output Economics.* New York: Oxford University Press, 1966.

LEROI-GOURHAN, ANDRÉ. "The Evolution of Paleolithic Art." *Scientific American,* February 1968, pp. 58–70.

———. *Treasures of Prehistoric Art.* New York: Abrams, 1967.

LOWES, JOHN LIVINGSTON. *The Road to Xanadu.* Boston: Houghton Mifflin, 1964.

LOWIE, ROBERT H. *Primitive Religion.* New York: Grosset and Dunlap. 1952.

LUMLEY, HENRY DE. "Les Fouilles de Terra Amata à Nice: Premiers Résultats." *Bulletin du Musée d'Anthropologie Préhistorique de Monaco* 13 (1966):29–51.

LUMLEY, HENRY DE. "A Paleolithic Camp at Nice." *Scientific American,* May 1969, pp. 42–50.

MARCUSE, HERBERT. *Eros and Civilization.* New York: Random House, 1962.

MARSHACK, ALEXANDER. "Lunar Notation on Upper Paleolithic Remains." *Science* 146 (1964):743–745.

———. "Cognitive Aspects of Upper Paleolithic Engraving." *Current Anthropology* 13 (1972):445–477.

———. *The Roots of Civilization.* New York: McGraw-Hill, 1972.

MARSHALL, D. S., and SUGGS, R. C., eds. *Human Sexual Behavior.* New York: Basic Books, 1971.

MARX, KARL. *Selected Writings in Sociology and Social Philosophy.* Edited by T. B. Bottomore and Maximilian Rubel. New York: McGraw-Hill, 1964.

MASLOW, A. H. *Motivation and Personality.* New York: Harper, 1954.

MEAD, MARGARET. *Coming of Age in Samoa.* New York: Morrow, 1930.

———. *Male and Female.* New York: Morrow, 1949.

MELLAART, JAMES. "Early Cultures of the South Anatolian Plateau." *Anatolian Studies* 11 (1961):158–184.

———. "Excavations at Çatal Hüyük: First Preliminary Report." *Anatolian Studies* 12 (1962):41–65.

———. "Excavations at Çatal Hüyük: Second Preliminary Report." *Anatolian Studies* 13 (1963):43–103.

———. "Excavations at Çatal Hüyük: Third Preliminary Report." *Anatolian Studies* 14 (1964):39–119.

———. "A Neolithic City in Turkey." *Scientific American,* September 1964, pp. 94–104.

———. "Excavations at Çatal Hüyük: Fourth Preliminary Report." *Anatolian Studies* 16 (1966):165–191.

———. "Çatal Hüyük West." *Anatolian Studies* 15 (1965):135–156.

———. *Earliest Civilizations of the Near East.* New York: McGraw-Hill, 1965.

———. "Çatal Hüyük—A Neolithic Town in Anatolia." In *New Aspects of Archaeology,* edited by Mortimer Wheeler. New York: McGraw-Hill, 1967.

———. "The Earliest Settlements in Western Asia from the Ninth to the End of the Fifth Millennium B.C." and "Anatolia Before 4000 B.C." In *The Cambridge Ancient History,* vol. 1, edited by I. E. S. Edwards, C. J. Gadd, and N. E. L. Hammond. Cambridge: Cambridge University Press, 1970.

MURDOCK, G. P. et al. "Ethnographic Atlas." *Ethnology* 1–6, 1962–1967.

NASH, MANNING. *Primitive and Peasant Economic Systems.* Chicago: Chandler, 1966.

NATIONAL ACADEMY OF SCIENCES. *Recommended Dietary Allowances.* Rev. ed. Publication 589. Washington: National Research Council, 1958.

O'KANE, WALTER C. *Sun in the Sky.* Norman: University of Oklahoma Press, 1950.

OSBORN, HENRY FAIRFIELD. *Proboscidea.* 2 vols. New York: American Museum Press of the American Museum of Natural History, 1942.

PEABODY, CHARLES. "Red Paint." *Journal de la Société des Américanistes de Paris,* n.s. 19 (1927):207–244.

PERKINS, DEXTER, JR., and DALY, PATRICIA. "A Hunter's Village in Neolithic Turkey." *Scientific American,* November 1968, pp. 96–106.

PIAGET, JEAN. *The Construction of Reality in the Child.* New York: Ballantine Books, 1971.

PIAGET, JEAN, and INHELDER, BARBEL. *The Psychology of the Child.* New York: Basic Books, 1969.

PIGGOTT, STUART. Introduction to *The Dawn of Civilization,* edited by Stuart Piggott. New York: McGraw-Hill, 1961.

PILBEAM, DAVID. *The Ascent of Man.* New York: Macmillan, 1972.

RADCLIFFE-BROWN, A. R. *The Andaman Islanders.* New York: Free Press, 1964.

RADIN, PAUL. *Primitive Religion.* New York: Dover, 1957.

READ, HERBERT, ed. *The Meaning of Art.* New York: Praeger, 1972.

REDFIELD, ROBERT. *The Primitive World and Its Transformations.* Ithaca, New York: Cornell University Press, 1953.

REED, CHARLES A. "Animal Domestication in the Prehistoric Near East." *Science* 130 (1955):1629–1639.

ROBBINS, MICHAEL G. "Material Culture and Cognition." In *Art and Aesthetics in Primitive Societies,* edited by Carol F. Jopling. New York: Dutton, 1971, pp. 328–334.

ROHEIM, GEZA. *The Origin and Function of Culture.* New York: Doubleday Anchor Books, 1971.

RYDER, M. L. "Report of Textiles from Çatal Hüyük." *Anatolian Studies* 15 (1965): 175–176.

SACHS, CURT. *Our Musical Heritage—A Short History of Music.* 2nd ed. Englewood Cliffs, N.J.: Prentice-Hall, 1955.

SAHLINS, M. D. *Tribesmen.* Englewood Cliffs, N.J.: Prentice-Hall, 1968.

SAHLINS, M. D., and SERVICE, E. R., eds. *Evolution and Culture.* Ann Arbor: University of Michigan Press, 1960.

SANDERSON, IVAN T. *The Dynasty of Abu.* New York: Knopf, 1962.

SAUER, CARL O. "Seashore—Primitive Home of Man?" *Proceedings of the American Philosophical Society* 106 (1962): 41–47.

SCHALLER, GEORGE B. *The Deer and the Tiger.* Chicago: University of Chicago Press, 1967.

SCHALLER, GEORGE B. and LOWTHER, GORDON R. "The Relevance of Carnivore Behavior to the Study of Early Hominids." *Southwestern Journal of Anthropology* 25 (1969):307–340.

SERVICE, E. R. *Primitive Social Organization.* New York: Random House, 1962.

———. *Profiles in Ethnology.* New York: Harper and Row, 1963.

———. *The Hunters.* Foundations of Modern Anthropology Series. Englewood Cliffs, N.J.: Prentice-Hall, 1966.

———. *Cultural Evolutionism—Theory in Practice.* New York: Holt, 1971.

SKINNER, B. F. *Verbal Behavior.* New York: Appleton, 1957.

SOLECKI, R. S. "Prehistory in Shanidar Valley, Northern Iraq," *Science* 139 (1963): 179–193.

STRUEVER, STUART, ed. *Prehistoric Agriculture*. American Museum of Natural History Sourcebooks in Anthropology. Garden City, N.Y.: Natural History Press, 1971.

TEILHARD DE CHARDIN, PIERRE. *The Phenomenon of Man*. New York: Harper and Row, 1959.

UCKO, PETER J. and DIMBLEBY, G. W., eds. *The Domestication and Exploitation of Plants and Animals*. Chicago: Aldine, 1969.

UCKO, PETER J., and ROSENFELD, ANDREE. *Paleolithic Cave Art*. New York: McGraw-Hill, 1967.

UNDERHILL, RUTH M. *Papago Indian Religion*. New York: Columbia University Press, 1946, pp. 211–242.

UNITED STATES DEPARTMENT OF AGRICULTURE. *Nutritive Value of Foods*. Home and Garden Bulletin no. 72. Washington: U.S. Department of Agriculture, 1960.

VESEY-FITZGERALD, D. F. "Grazing Succession Among East African Game Animals." *Journal of Mammalogy* 41 (1960):161–172.

VON FURER-HAIMENDORF, CHRISTOPH. *Morals and Merit*. Chicago: University of Chicago Press, 1967.

———. *The Konyak Nagas: An American Frontier Tribe*. Case Studies in Cultural Anthropology. New York: Holt, 1969.

WALLACE, A. F. C. *Culture and Personality*. New York: Random House, 1961.

WERTIME, THEODORE A. "Man's First Encounters with Metallurgy." *Science* 146 (1964):1257–1267.

WHITE, LESLIE A. *The Acoma Indians*. 47th Annual Report, 1929/30. Washington: U.S. Bureau of Indian Ethnology, 1932, pp. 17–192.

———. *The Evolution of Culture—The Development of Civilization to the Fall of Rome*. New York: McGraw-Hill, 1959.

Index

About the Author

Walter A. Fairservis, Jr., is professor of the department of Anthropology and Sociology at Vassar College, Poughkeepsie, New York, and acting curator of the Eurasian Anthropology Collections at the American Museum of Natural History, New York. He has been director of the American Museum field expeditions to Afghanistan, Pakistan, Egypt, India, and Iran and is presently director of the archaeological expedition in Allahdino in South Pakistan. His books include *Origins of Oriental Civilizations, The Ancient Kingdoms of the Nile,* and *The Roots of Ancient India.*